Broken Hallelujah Love Note is the sequel to *Broken Hallelujah: 40 Days in the Wilderness.*

Matt and MK invite you into their lives as they figure out a new life together. *Love Note* is a true story about the trials and adjustments of an anoxic brain injury survivor and her family.

ISBN: 9781671987388

Love Note is written from the perspective of MK and what she remembers transpired while regaining her abilities after an anoxic brain injury.

We dedicate this book to all the families and their loved ones who need hope: hope that there's more to this journey than what is visible. Every journey is different. Never give up trying to find a new normal; don't stop trying.

Thank you, Matt, Aubrey, and Emily for finding a way.

Table of Contents

ONE

Ain't Going Back to Rehab ... 27

TWO

The Drive Home ... 30

THREE

Home ...   32

FOUR

Everything Changes ... 38

FIVE

The Chair ... 41

SIX

Night Terrors ... 46

SEVEN

Matt ... 50

EIGHT

Finding a Way ... 53

NINE

First Morning Home ... 58

TEN

Banana Pancakes ... 60

ELEVEN

Birds ... 63

TWELVE

Gift of Being ... 67

THIRTEEN

Where's Mary? ... 71

FOURTEEN

What, No Horn?... 76

FIFTEEN

Nightmares ... 82

SIXTEEN

Matt ... 85

SEVENTEEN

New Day, New Chance ... 88

EIGHTEEN

Outpatient Rehab ... 97

NINETEEN

Case Manager... 102

TWENTY

Speech Therapy ... 110

TWENTY-ONE

Physical Therapy ... 116

TWENTY-TWO

Occupational Therapy ... 122

TWENTY-THREE

First Outing ... 131

TWENTY-FOUR

Family Decisions ... 136

TWENTY-FIVE

Despair ... 140

TWENTY-SIX

Love Is a Verb ... 146

TWENTY-SEVEN

Paralyzed with Fear ... 153

TWENTY-EIGHT

3:30 a.m. Matt ... 155

TWENTY-NINE

Day of Decisions... 158

THIRTY

DR. G ... 166

THIRTY-ONE

Tenderly ... 176

THIRTY-TWO

Emily Leaves for College ... 181

THIRTY-THREE

It's Too Quiet ... 189

THIRTY-FOUR

Fear ... 199

THIRTY-FIVE

Matt ... 205

THIRTY-SIX

More Rehab ... 209

THIRTY-SEVEN

A Social Gathering ... 220

THIRTY-EIGHT

Date Night Disaster ... 224

THIRTY-NINE

Medical Marijuana ... 230

FORTY

Ginger ... 237

FORTY-ONE

Doctor Aubrey ... 245

FORTY-TWO

Green ... 254

FORTY-THREE

Choices Cannot be Undone ... 260

FORTY-FOUR

Love Notes ... 267

FORTY-FIVE

Six Months of Trying ... 271

FORTY-SIX

Finding Me ... 274

FORTY-SEVEN

No More Walker ... 279

FORTY-EIGHT

Words and Actions ... 283

FORTY-NINE

Dream of Independence ... 287

FIFTY

It's Okay to Fail ... 289

FIFTY-ONE

Sunday Mornings ... 292

FIFTY-TWO

Tears Shed ... 298

FIFTY-THREE

Red like Roses ... 301

FIFTY-FOUR

Silence ... 304

FIFTY-FIVE

I'm Here! ... 308

FIFTY-SIX

Butterflies ... 313

FIFTY-SEVEN

Jesus is the Light ... 321

FIFTY-EIGHT

That's What She Said ... 324

FIFTY-NINE

God Blessed Us with Humor ... 328

SIXTY

Same Old Story, Same Old Me ... 331

SIXTY-ONE

Garden of The Gods ... 334

SIXTY-TWO

Elves, or ... 341

SIXTY-THREE

Music Therapy ... 344

SIXTY-FOUR

Going Back ... 352

SIXTY-FIVE

Hope ... 356

Acknowledgements

Preface

Broken Hallelujah Love Note is the sequel to *Broken Hallelujah: 40 Days in The Wilderness.*

This story picks up from leaving the safety and security of inpatient rehabilitation after 40 days of immense changes to the new journey home where everyone has a job to do to ensure proper care of MK.

We want to share with you how a family member's brain injury not only affects the person who acquires the disability but the family dynamic as well. Decisions were the forefront of family discussions and the girls, Aubrey and Emily, made the most difficult decision of them all. Who would put their life on hold to help? After the two of them worked it out and confirmed with Matt, they decided that Emily would go back to school, and Aubrey would move back home and do everything she could to help.

Emily was a sophomore at Florida International University on a generous beach volleyball scholarship. She would call every day after beach

volleyball practice. On the night of November 21, 2013, I (MK) was having a difficult time speaking. She asked what was going on. I explained that my leg had swollen and felt warm. Emily asked if this was the same side on which I had sprained my ankle. If so, she said, I needed to go to the hospital because it could be a blood clot. I assured her I was seeing a doctor in the morning and would be sure to mention it then.

This was the last conversation I remember having until December 3, the day I woke up to my husband, Matt, singing to me.

Emily got a call a few hours after our phone conversation and flew home immediately. The outlook was grim. I had already coded once when they called her. By the time she could arrive at the hospital, I was in ICU. I had coded two more times. The doctors explained that I was more than likely brain dead. Emily, Aubrey, Matt, and a few relatives took shifts staying with me, not wanting me to be alone when I woke up.

Emily didn't want to go back to school. Matt assured her I would want her to go back. She did. It was difficult for her. She called several times a day to make sure everyone was okay.

During Christmas break, I was in inpatient rehab. I think Emily spent most of her break with me learning how to help me. I was an infant in an adult body, having to relearn how to walk, eat, and speak.

On December 31, they released me to go home in the care of my family.

Emily and Aubrey worked on helping me find a new normal. Emily left for school and called me every day, forcing me to talk. The significant anoxic brain injury affected my speech and motor skills. When she came home, she would record video exercises for me and help me with my writing. As part of my memory therapy, she would have me remember a simple joke and repeat it back to her. I'm sure this is how the telephone game was invented.

At a time in her life when she should have been taking chances, making mistakes, and getting messy, she stood beside me, Matt, and Aubrey.

This is our oldest daughter, Aubrey. My life-changing event also put her on a new, unplanned path. She quit college and stayed home to help care for me. She decided to put her young life on hold, to become my voice. This was not a simple decision, and it wasn't an easy one, but love prevails.

 I am now fairly independent, and Aubrey is now fulfilling her dreams.

She is finding the beauty in living a free life full of obstacles she has already  conquered. I recently asked her if she would do it all over again, knowing how much of a challenge it was. Without hesitation, she said, "Yes."

After suffering a pulmonary embolism that caused cardiac arrest three times, I had permanent brain damage. No one knew the extent, whether the damage was irreversible or how much ability I could regain. Both long-term and short-term memories affected. My speech was the most noticeable. Communication was difficult. But Matt didn't want me anywhere else but next to him.

I was an infant in an adult body. As my family celebrated that I was still alive, I struggled with the what ifs: the nightmares of the past and the fear of the future.

They loaded me in our two-door black Honda Civic from inpatient rehab and we began our greatest and most challenging journey together as a family. They would have to reteach me how to live, help me find a new normal. No one could predict what that would be like, but somehow, they all believed there was more in me, more that could be done.

The Podschweit family invites you to join them in the lowest of lows and the highest of highs as they discover what it means to love unconditionally, to have hope in the unseen even while experiencing fear of the reality of what has taken place.

They invite you to breathe in the nightmares MK faced and the demons that continue to haunt her. Learn from MK as she struggles with the reality of being disabled and what her new life looks like. Hope with her for what she longs her life to be.

From outbursts of anger to waterfalls of tears and everything in between. MK's life, her new life, is more than just existing, but a life of many failures and successes because her family never let her give up.

Pictured Emily, MK, Matt and Aubrey

Introduction

I, MK, coded (died) three times starting the evening of November 21, 2013, through early November 22, 2013. This story is a continuation of *Broken Hallelujah: 40 Days in The Wilderness*, of learning how to live with a brain injury: overcoming obstacles and grieving what once was.

I struggle with false memories from my time in ICU. They seem so very real, nightmares come to life. I mourn what once was and tried to figure out life with a brain injury. My thought processes turn on and off like a slow computer. I'm trying to navigate life in a dense fog. I have lost the ability to motivate myself, but I have a family that believes there is more in me than what I can share. It's through their unyielding love, the bonds of husband and wife, mother and daughter, that I find my strength to try.

Book One, Broken Hallelujah: 40 Days in the Wilderness, Chapter 30

Love Wins

December 29

As I was preparing for my final days in rehab, I wanted to be sure and thank everyone for their attention and help. When I asked if I could thank Mary personally for her care during the night shift, they looked puzzled and explained that they didn't have a Mary working. I just smiled and closed my eyes and thanked God for Mary, my angel.

Emily and Aubrey worked on helping me find a new normal. During Christmas break, I think Emily spent most of her time learning how to help me.

As part of my memory therapy, Emily would have me remember a simple joke or something from watching Ellen and repeat it back to her. (I am sure this is how the telephone game was invented!) She did this at a time in her life when she should have been taking chances, making mistakes, and getting messy, but there she stood beside me!

I am forever grateful for the encouragement, love, and unyielding support that both Aubrey and Emily have given to me.

Matt's Blog: Mary Kaye's Odyssey

Sunday, December 29, 2013

Posted December 29, 2013, 10:40 p.m. by Matthew Podschweit. [Updated December 29, 2013, 10:40 p.m.]

It has been a long time since my last post, but please don't think not much has been happening. MK has been working so hard at physical and occupational therapy, and it's all about to pay off. Her discharge date of December 31 is still in force, and if you ask her, MK will tell you it can't come soon enough! This is not a reflection of the care she is receiving at Penrose Main Hospital—in fact, I think MK would agree that we will miss the wonderful people that have been instrumental in getting her prepared to come home.

Each day of therapy brings more and more progress. MK spent so much time in ICU, much of it on a ventilator. Many of her muscles, including her diaphragm, have atrophied to a certain extent. Dr. Guerrero, one of MK's doctors for rehab, reminded us that she may have spent as much as twelve minutes without a constant supply of oxygen to her brain. While her MRI did not show any permanent brain damage, that kind of injury will take time and effort to heal. Right now, MK can perform basic, everyday tasks and is walking very well with the assistance of a walker or cane. Her speech has been most noticeably affected. Physically, her time with the breathing tube has damaged her vocal cords and the muscles in her throat. Her voice is very quiet and breathy, and she needs to put forth much effort to project. She also became frustrated, as vocalizing what is in her mind is sometimes very difficult. We have been assured that none of this is necessarily permanent and that time and patience along with hard work in therapy will restore MK's abilities.

Throughout this chapter, our family has been the recipient of extraordinary grace and generosity. Expressions of love in the form of prayers and well-wishes, calls and visits, offers of service and help, and providence of food and money have overwhelmed and humbled us beyond my ability to express. Our deepest, heartfelt thanks go out to the many families and friends who have come alongside and shouldered this effort with us.

I resist the temptation to refer to our current situation as a "burden" or a "tragedy" because it is not as long as we think otherwise. Every day brings new opportunities to nurture relationships, to encourage and uplift each other and foster an environment of love and cooperation. To allow ourselves to become mired in woe and self-pity would undermine what I consider being the most worthwhile purpose of our lives—to sacrificially infuse love as an antidote into a culture that is poisoning itself with greed, selfishness, and hate. It starts at home, and I choose to love MK more tomorrow than I did today, and (thankfully) she chooses to do the same to me. I'd be hard-pressed to find anything to complain about.

It occurred to me that as MK returns home, it might be a good idea to ask her to take over this blog. I'll let you know her answer in a future post—please stay tuned.

Love wins!

BOOK 2

Chapter 1

Ain't Going Back to Rehab

On December 31, 2013, we left the rehabilitation center as a family: Matt, Aubrey, Emily, and me. The impatience in the air was palpable. The three of them, Matt with our very excited daughters, came early in the morning, after breakfast. Meanwhile, I still had to go through the torture of rehab to finish the last day of inpatient therapy. As this was going on, Dr. House went over the final care instructions with my family.

The first obstacle was to decide on home care.

I was never to be alone.

A rehabilitation facility or an in-home health care professional was suggested. This suggestion made me break down and cry.

Matt understood. He assured Dr. House that he would find a way without either of those solutions. Both girls immediately volunteered to stay home and care for me, to become a chauffeur, an interpreter with the doctors, our family's cook and rehabilitation coach while Matt eased his way back to work.

How could anyone possibly say thank you for such loving care? They had made many sacrifices for me. I felt very undeserving of such love and devotion, almost to the point of self-loathing. Dr. House explained that out-of-place emotions are part of the process. In fact, he was glad to see the tears.

Aubrey and Emily shared their feelings that this was nothing that Matt or I would not have done for them. Everyone was very reassuring that it would work out. Matt asked me to trust him, to focus on what needed to be done in my daily routine. They would take care of the rest.

Chapter 2
The Drive Home

The four of us piled into our 2-door black Honda Civic with the common gray walker, fashionable gait belt, and gifts that had accumulated over the past forty days. It felt good to leave. No—it felt fantastic!

They buckled me in and off we went on the road to home. Home! What an incredible word. Gazing straight ahead, I was only half-aware of a world outside the comfort of the car. The girls talked excitedly in the back seat. Matt had one hand on the wheel, the other alternated between the almost soundless changing of gears and holding my hand.

Chapter 3
Home

Home. Love. Are they the same? For me, at that moment, they loved me. I was home. We pulled into our two-car garage in the long and narrow townhouse we were renting. It was a cream-colored stucco—like every townhome in our division. Most had three units attached. Ours was tucked in the middle, stretching some thirty feet back. Neighbors happily waved hello when we pulled up to the garage. Matt smiled and waved cheerfully in return.

With constant reminders to lift my legs, they assisted me out of the car. One step up and we were all in the kitchen. It was a rather smooth transition from the garage.

Our home smelled fresh, clean, well taken care of. Magoo, my beta fish of two years, had a clean bowl and was eagerly swimming around, waiting for his food.

We made our way through the kitchen as Matt guided me on a tour of our house. First was our bedroom on the left. Because of not being able to trust my balance, Matt had placed a chair to block the downstairs entryway. I was thankful for the tour, the hand on the back of the gait belt, and the little things the girls and Matt would show me. Everything that should have been done to provide safety and security was done.

Our home is rooms and walls like any other, yet it is only the love there that matters. The walls are smiles and filled with laughter, decorated with pictures of the people who hold my heart. Christmas decorations adorned the house and presents waited under the tree. While we dwell here, this home is so much more than the sum of its parts and for that, I have love to thank, the glue of my existence. Love. To be loved by Matt, Aubrey, and Emily is all that mattered, is all that matters.

I tried hard to remember what our downstairs looked like. Our girls enjoyed their own space when they were home. They enjoyed playing Mario Kart and laughing, having friends over, yet, I couldn't remember what it looked like. They all began reminiscing. Matt said, "Honey, remember?" I smiled and nodded my head.

Our bedroom was very spacious, a master suite with heavy beige carpet throughout the room. It wasn't easy to maneuver in the walker; it was exhausting. Matt hung on snugly to the gait belt as we made our way through the bedroom. I was being intentional about lifting my feet. I was also beginning to feel overwhelmed but still had things to see.

In the Master Suite was a private bathroom. Long and narrow. To the right was a whirlpool tub that had not seen a naked body in months. The dust covering the faucet was noticeable. I used to love hot baths, to soak, to escape. Did anyone else enjoy this luxury, or was it too difficult for anyone in my family to take some time for themselves? The heartache of what my family had been through was difficult to bear. I took deep breaths to hold back the sorrow, the self-pity, the emotions. The thought of lying in a tub of hot water, soaking up the aroma of lavender, brought a sense of ease to the day, but there was no way I could step in, sit down, or hold myself up without the fear of falling, without the fear of not being strong enough to push up. This is something that will be a gift, a present of celebration. A bath is now on my list of desires.

Past the whirlpool bathtub was his, and hers sinks on opposite sides of the room. A private toilet area was located on the right. Matt had made the toilet handicapped accessible with a riser and handles on each side. The shower was on the left side. Matt opened the shower door and showed me the seat and safety bars he had installed. He was trying hard to make me feel comfortable. He had thought of everything to ensure my safety. At the very end of this elongated room, through sliding doors, was our walk-in closet. Work clothes were still hanging in the bags from the cleaners, dresses and dress shoes were still in the same place I had left them forty days ago. Forty days. I burst into tears; I couldn't contain the flooding of emotion any longer.

Matt held me and asked what was wrong. Finally, I could tell him in a broken whisper, "I wonder which dress you would have used to bury me in."

There was nothing he could say.

Chapter 4
Everything Changes

Handicapped accessible. Matt had been working hard to ensure my safety and comfort. He had thought everything through, with safety being his number one concern.

Although, that is a heavy word to say, to think, to believe: *handicapped*. Forty days ago, we were planning our first practice with a 12U volleyball team; I was a fun-loving mother, wife, and coach. Now, now our world has changed forever as we try to navigate what life will be like with an anoxic brain injury and how to accommodate a handicapped wife. Our lives, as lucky as we were, would change, ever evolving into a new life, a new beginning.

I was feeling overwhelmed. Matt could sense this and escorted me into the living room. I used my walker as he gently reminded me to lift my feet while he hung on to my gait belt. My left side quaked. Every few steps I would take using the walker, my brain would reset. Matt would remind me it was okay; it would take time.

The house had an open floor plan. Only a half wall separated the kitchen from the dining room which opened to the family room. With high vaulted ceilings, and the cream-colored walls decorated with family pictures and holiday cheer. The Christmas tree stood 12 feet tall, with flickering lights on just for me. At the end of this room was a glass patio door attached to a small enclosed deck. Off the deck was a long line of pine trees. Matt shared it was a favorite place of mine to sit outside on the deck listening to the birds. He saw my confusion and briefly said, "Not today love, it's too cold outside."

Chapter 5
The Chair

Matt lead me toward the black leather chair, the chair in which forty days ago, he had propped me up before

leaving for volleyball practice. The black leather recliner that was a gift from Grandma Judy. It used to be Grandpa Phil's, but he recently passed away. Phil's gone. I mourned and celebrated the great man, silently thanked him for being with me, for encouraging me to go back. And all that is left of his legacy in our home, the chair. This black leather recliner that we all loved, my favorite chair. A chair that used to be very inviting. A chair that is so comfortable, so cozy with a small pillow and blanket. It was calling for me. Calling for me to sit for a while and put my feet up. This chair saved my life. It kept my feet elevated which slowed the movement of the blood clot. It kept me safe and encased me with its arms, ensuring I would not fall. I began crying. Matt leaned over and kissed my forehead. With no words, he knew what was going on. He sensed the fear that was radiating all around me.

He turned on the gas fireplace with a quick flick of the switch on the wall and sat me down on the loveseat. The fireplace was encased in stucco and still had the Christmas garland draped around the mantel.

Four stockings hung from Christmas Day, stockings filled with gifts and surprises. Aubrey and Emily wanted to open presents together, so they had waited, patiently waiting for me to come home. They filled the remaining mantel space with a television and a DVD player. Matt kept all the electronics off so I could adjust to being home. It was silence with a purpose.

The girls spent time downstairs giving Matt and me time to adjust, to enjoy the quiet together. The day turned into darkness. The feel of him holding me in our home was like a little touch of heaven: warm, together, cozy. If there was a way to extend the time just so I could have stayed close to him for a little longer, feeling safe in his embrace, we would have grasped it. To be loved, and cherished, is something to delight in.

His arms wrapped tight around me, bringing a warm sense of peace. I had longed for this moment. A calming of the storms in my heart. Bright hope for the future. In his embrace. My left side moved violently and still; Matt held me. I started to believe that there was nothing out there to fear, snuggled in the cradle of his arms. Much-needed sleep swept me away.

Somehow, he tucked me into bed for an early night. My brain had shut down. There was too much to process. They kept the house quiet.

Chapter 6
Night Terrors

January 1, 2014. Sleep would have to wait. Insomnia is the companion that won't quit. The fear of closing my eyes took on life. Matt is my safety, my harbor, my balance; no matter where I am, if he is with me, I would somehow understand what is real, understand what the assurance of living is, of love. But I struggled with reality. *Am I alive?* Hopelessness came charging at me in waves of undeniable emotion, directly assaulting my head and heart.

Matt held me and that seemed to help, but the nightmares persisted. In the middle of the night, the feeling of being tied down, unable to breathe, of being lost and confused was ever present. That moment seemed so real. There was an invisible hand clasped over my mouth and nose; my ribs heaved as if bound by ropes, straining to inflate my lungs. My limbs felt tied. The feeling of being paralyzed was frightening as the struggle with reality was tipping in death's direction.

Fear. How do I explain the unexplainable? I was spinning out of control, being pushed into blackness. I wanted to run; wanted to scream, "I am here! I am here!" and yet I lay in frozen sweat.

Matt's touch and soothing whispers of "You are home, you are safe," are reassuring, inviting, warm, and drove me back into the present. He tried to wrestle the left side of my body as it's in an uncontrollable, thrashing rage of violence.

The negative memories came with a cost. Living a false reality when I closed my eyes for some much-needed rest was terrifying. No one should be fearful of sleep, yet I was. Every nightmare seemed real. Every nightmare took me back to a place where I didn't want to go, where I didn't want to remember. There was nothing of value in them.

Sleep seemed like a very distant reality. I wanted to sleep; I longed for it, but it would not come tonight.

Tonight, I lay in a sweat-drenched cocoon, tonight. It would be a long night.

Chapter 7

Matt

A memory of that first night home. It's 3:30 in the morning and MK is crazed. Her left side is moving violently, her eyes have frozen over like the surface of a winter lake, robbing them of their usual warmth. She's in there, I know it, but it's like she just took a huge step back from life. I want to reach in and tell her it isn't hopeless. I whisper, "You are home. You are safe," over and over again until her breathing stabilizes, and her eyes show a glimmer of life. The doctors had warned me, had tried to prepare me for her night terrors, but now I have just witnessed them. I cry, holding my precious jewel, wondering what she is running from, what pain she was hiding inside. The panic is visible on her face, the anguish, the fear. I wish it would go away. I know that's a selfish want, I miss my Mary, the fun-loving rock star, my wife. I didn't know how rocky the road was in front of us, I only knew I would be by her side and coach her into getting up again. She needed rest, a good night's sleep, uninterrupted slumber. I just don't know how to help except hold her.

Chapter 8
Finding a way

It was early morning. Everything seemed sad and slow. The only windows we had in our bedroom faced west. There was no morning light. I wasn't sure if Matt got much sleep. He was always checking on me, trying desperately to keep my left side from thrashing, from taking on a life of its own.

I had to have a game plan for getting my life back, if not for my sake, then for that of my husband, my forever friend, my lover. Weariness was setting in. We'd walked through forty days of the unknown. Although we were celebrating my homecoming, we had to find a new way of life, for now anyway. I desperately searched to find the missing link between self and me, realizing peace could only be found once I had found myself. As corny as it sounds, it's an important piece of existence. Self. Finding self.

Once I knew who I was, who I wanted to be, and where I wanted to go, I knew I could not settle for what I had become, for the love and loyalty I have for Matt. I knew I could not see him tied down or tied up trying his very best to take care of me. I just didn't know how to get there. It was all so overwhelming. Nothing would happen without adequate sleep and that would not come easily. I could think these thoughts. I, however, could not speak them aloud or provide the action to take.

I lay quietly, waiting patiently for help to get up out of bed for the day. I could not speak the words "Good Morning!" unable to help myself. UGH! I had been given the gift to live again, to love; how could I accept this new way of living? Everything is temporary; I was not willing to accept this as my new normal, our new normal. Moments like these seemed to last for eternity. I thought about people who did not have the love or help I was blessed with and began to weep silent tears. I hated that crying was my go-to emotion. I wished I could control it. It brought heartache to my family, who don't deserve my emotional rollercoaster.

As I lay there, I imagined the tears shed in our home that once was full of life, of laughter. Everyone now seemed cautious and in a continuous state of wondering. I couldn't help but cry, thinking of my family's desperate prayers. Everyone seemed frozen with the looming question as what to do next, how to help. The clatter of pots and pans came from the kitchen, as did the aroma of pancakes and freshly brewed coffee. My stomach began to rumble. How do I communicate? I have no way of saying, "I am awake," so I lay there trying to will my left side to stop moving, to relax.

When Matt came into the room to help me for the day, he was heartbroken to see my tearful expression. In my sadness there was no past or future. I was just living by the moment, the moment of waking into this new reality. My mind wandered trying to remember, trying to live, to love freely again, without hesitation. *I have a long way to go and I don't know how I will get my old life back.* My old life? Wait, this is my life. The only way I could express myself is through tears.

Chapter 9
First Morning Home

Matt, so kind, came in to help me begin my day. A new day, my first day home. Quietly he helped me to the bathroom and carefully dressed me in baggy clothes after a quick sponge bath, just underwear, no bra yet. The bruises from CPR mottled my torso; it was still very sensitive. My attire was an oversized sweatshirt, black pull-up pants, extra-soft black ankle socks, and black tennis shoes he double knotted. Gait belt attached, walker set in front of me, my sweet Matt switched hats from husband to the physical therapist. He did the best he could with what we had; no complaints on my part. We made our way to the delicious smells from the kitchen.

Aubrey and Emily had made breakfast. Banana pancakes, bacon, and coffee. He sat me down at our table, the size of a wagon wheel, made of wrought iron and glass. Around the table were four chairs, plates, napkins, and silverware. It was a beautiful setting, and I was so thankful I could share a meal at home, prepared with love. Matt helped move me closer to the table.

Chapter 10
Banana Pancakes

The girls set plates filled with banana pancakes, hot bacon, and steaming cups of coffee on the table. One look and I tried hard to keep my fear at bay, to hide the emotions of confusion and disappointment, not with my family, but with myself. I didn't understand what was going on. I kept my head down and my gaze on the floor. I couldn't look at the food. I just sat there dazed and confused, trying to hold back the sorrow. This emotion tried hard to rear its confusing head. For me, it had quickly become my unwanted friend.

Matt was trying to comfort me. Aubrey came over and started rubbing my arm. Emily gently asked, "Mom, what's wrong?" When I tried to explain that the food confused me, Matt remembered his conversation with Dr. House. Dr. House said that with brain injuries it's common to have a food sensitivity. Taste, smell, texture, even color can be very confusing.

He looked at the plate of food and asked Emily to remove the bacon from the plate and to add creamer to my coffee, diminishing the rich tone of freshly brewed coffee to that of, well, a little coffee with my creamer. The pancakes, bananas, and butter were of the same color scheme. That seemed to work. Breakfast was delicious. I wished I could do more, but Matt insisted they would figure it out and for me not to worry.

The four of us sat there eating. Laughter was spontaneous and joy filled the room. Aubrey and Emily kept the meal lively and entertaining, sharing stories of their lives these past 40 days that I have missed. They were careful not to speak about the nightmare they lived while I was in ICU, but I could feel the heartache they tried to hide; I could sense their fear of tomorrow and all I could do was smile and nod my head.

Chapter 11
Birds

After breakfast, Matt moved me to the loveseat, close to the window so I could look outside and watch for birds. I sat quietly and watched in wonder as the bird on the branch in the

evergreen tree moved its head from side to side. Every turn was rapid. But in the moments, it was still; it looked at me with its glossy black eyes set in the plumage of grays and browns. The bird was small, no bigger than a pinecone. I could not remember what we called them. I knew it was a common bird with a high-pitched chirp, usually found in groups. *Come on brain, you know this; you know this.* I glanced up. Emily looked mournful with her eyes fixed on my face. Could she read the expressions of self-loathing and confusion? She said my name: "Mama," and I blinked back into the now and refocused my frustration into joy at seeing my youngest daughter alongside me. Emily came over with a hairbrush to assist in my preparation for the day. She saw the familiar tune of turmoil strewn over my face as I sat there with reddened cheeks as the bird flew away. Freedom. Freedom. Oh, how I wished for freedom.

Emily gently said, "Are you not happy, Mama?"

I couldn't share with her what I wanted to ask. I didn't know how to, so I smiled sweetly and nodded my head.

The next thing I remember was Matt's phone call to rehab. His words echoed in my head, "I need your advice."

I had filled their lives with worry, wonder, heartache, and celebration. They had to adjust to life without me while I was being cared for by the hospital staff. And now that I was home, the responsibility of my care had fallen in their laps. As excited as they were to have me at home, the question of *What do we do now?* Was heavy on their hearts.

When Matt got off the phone with the rehabilitation center, he and the girls all sat down next to me. He explained that I had outpatient rehab the next morning. Today was a day for adjustments, for family and celebrations!

"You have no expectations here; we will take care of you, and honey, it's okay to cry. Dr. House has explained your brain is healing and to expect the shedding of tears. You can't control your emotions so it's okay if you cry. We promise we won't take it personally."

I smiled and nodded my head.

Chapter 12

Gift of Being

"The girls have been waiting to open gifts, sweetie. Are you ready? I can help you."

I smiled and nodded my head. I have no memory of what gifts were given, no memory of what anyone received. My focus was not on the material but the gift of being. Of being the wife to Matt. The mother to Aubrey and Emily. They blessed me. I was loved and thankfully I had a chance to love them.

Matt said, "While the girls are cleaning the kitchen, let's call our families. Everyone has been so excited for us."

He began with my mom. She was giddy with excitement, seriously could not contain her joy. She burst into a celebration. Like a yawn that's contagious, her celebration made me laugh. Joy! Every small thing in life is a moment able to nourish the soul if we let joy in. JOY! To live in a moment encased with awe and humbleness, to embrace the gift of life. Let it fill you to the brim, so much that your joy will overflow and make better the lives of all around you. These are the joyful moments. "Thanks for loving me!" I whispered.

Judy Murphy, my mother-in-law, was already on her way down to Colorado Springs from Idaho Springs. She was always up for a celebration plus the girls always love being around her. She has a way of making everything all right. A gift that Matt has inherited. A soothing presence.

After saying goodbye to Mom, I remembered what kind of bird was in the evergreen tree outside our window, the bird with the glassy black eyes that sparkled with curiosity, with wonder.

I whispered out loud, not meaning to draw attention, just was trying to say it on my own. "Sssppp," *deep breath, try again*, "sspppaaarrr..." My eyes filled with a celebration of excitement.

Matt moved in closer, I pointed outside and Matt immediately finished my thoughts. "Sparrow?" he said.

I smiled and nodded my head yes.

"That's right, honey, you like to watch the birds. Did you see a sparrow?"

I smiled and nodded my head yes as a hoarse whisper escaped: "Yessss."

Chapter 13
Where's Mary?

How could I work if I couldn't live? The message from Jesus echoed in my head, "You must go back, your job is not done?"

The next call was to my brothers Danny and David. Matt did the talking for us. Everyone was happy I was home.

I hated feeling like a burden. The guilt was heavy on my heart and with my stupid brain injury; I had a difficult time recognizing what was real. What had I done to deserve such love? How could I make up for the heartache, the sadness that I dragged everyone close to me through? I prayed silently. Was God listening? Had he left me? Mary had not come to my rescue last night. Was she real, was I alive? Or was this a cruel form of hell? I prayed for mercy. I didn't feel like I deserved the love of our Father, Son, and Holy Ghost, but I clung to it and hung onto the shreds of faith, onto my conversation with him: "Your job is not done." I had to believe at that moment; I had to trust Him. My redeemer. How could I possibly work when I couldn't live? *God, please show me or take me but please help me out of this lukewarm life, out of this gray dreariness.* I promised myself, I promised God: *Whatever it would take to get better, whatever it takes, I will work hard, I will. I will. I will.*

I then told Matt, the best way I could, that I wanted to help. The harder I tried to communicate, the more my left side took on a life of its own. He saw the frustration. He recognized my will, my competitive spirit. There would be no rest. I was diving into our home life headfirst and he needed to teach me how to swim.

He concerned himself about my left side being so uncontrollable. That would be an obstacle to overcome. We talked about putting my left side in a sling, but Dr. House explained that a sling wouldn't control the involuntary muscle movement. It might make things worse. Worse??? I was not sure how. I just had to help I didn't want this feeling of insignificance of being a burden.

Matt and the girls made a grocery list to make sure that my food was the same color and without a lot of texture. Today I wanted yellow and cream and orange colors. Today.

We did not understand how long this would take, this color and texture phobia, this new fear of what? I did not understand that this was a precursor to healing; I just knew that it was challenging to even look at food with color and different textures. For now, Aubrey, Emily, and Matt didn't show any hesitation to help with this request.

Aubrey stayed home with me while Matt and Emily went to Walmart for groceries.

My sweet, sweet Aubrey. She kept my mind engaged with sharing about her days, work, and friends. I laughed when she told a funny story about school and work and getting to the hospital before they locked her out. I just couldn't help but laugh. Then, like a flicker of a faulty switch, I began to cry. I was trying to apologize that they left her to care for me. My dearest child hugged me and gently joked, "Well, Mom, where else would I rather be?" At that moment her arms squeezed a fraction tighter, and she kissed me on my forehead. This was life, real life. Matt's message to the family echoed in her thoughts: 'Mom's not in control of her emotions.' But Aubrey couldn't control her sobs. She whispered in my ear, 'I'm glad you are still here, Mom. I'm so glad."

Matt and Emily made a quick trip. When they came home, Matt had a surprise for me: a basket for my walker.

Chapter 14
What, No Horn?

The basket was nothing fancy, just a sturdy heavy-duty basket. He had bought some zip-ties and Emily had picked out a few silk flowers. They began decorating my basket. I asked, "Where's the horn?" Everyone laughed, first, because they understood what I was asking and second, because of a conversation Em and Matt had had at the store. Both thought a horn would be hilarious, but on second thought, they could see me taking advantage of it. Emily laughed, pretending to be me in my walker, beeping my way around the house. It was funny. To laugh at me felt good, it felt right. Matt asked, "Anyone up for a movie?" Just then Grandma Judy came to the door.

The girls both ran to greet her. She filled their lives, our lives, with amazing hugs and huge smiled. She brought dinner for everyone. Matt had let her know about my intolerance to color and texture, so she made homemade macaroni and cheese, cheesy garlic bread, and yellow wax beans.

Okay, so the meal wasn't health conscious, but it was delicious. But more than that, the happiness at the table, the laughter, the reviving joy was exactly what I needed. I am certain it is what we all needed. Love wins, always. As difficult as the road was ahead of us, that night, that night, we had a reprieve. A break from the fear. That night as I sat there, at our table, it filled my heart with love and gratitude. I refused to surrender to the panic that tried desperately to escape. I would have to learn how to enjoy these moments of sunshine, these beautiful moments of freedom, of loss of self. And learn to live in the moment of joy, happiness, laughter, and love.

After dinner, sensing it overwhelmed me, Matt guided me to our loveseat. He asked Mom and the girls to wait on cleaning up the kitchen. Every noise echoed in our open-plan house. The clamoring of pots, pans, and dirty dishes was loud and frankly obnoxious. We all sat down in the quiet. Matt cradled me in his arms and asked if I was ready for that movie. He picked out something safe: *White Christmas*. All five of us sat down together. The fireplace was on; the aroma from dinner wafted throughout the house. Mom snuggled up in the beloved black recliner, the girls grabbed two pillows and a throw and camped out on the floor, each with an excited bounce with every step, every motion. They were giddy with joy. A day they could only dream of, a day they would talk about; today, tonight, we were all under the same roof. Twenty-four hours into my first day home. To see them so happy brought so much hope, so much excitement, so much wonderment. I began to shed these tears of joy, allowing them to fall freely as they cascaded down my face.

Matt looked at me and smiled. He reached for me and gently pulled my face toward him with his warm hand.

He lovingly kissed my eyes. When he tasted the saltiness, he smiled. His smile. His tender touch, his warm embrace. *If I have his smile, his touch, I know I can do this. Oh, Matty, I know that I am loved.* Cradled in his arms, secure, we began watching *White Christmas.* I closed my eyes and fell asleep. My left side still moved violently, but with Matt's firm embrace, he could securely nestle me into his warm grasp and envelop all the struggles, the doubt, the fear.

Here, in the now, in the present, I have been blessed with the opportunity to make positive memories. Yes, positive memories, they are good and nourishing, supportive and kind. Making new memories with the people I love. This way I become confident and appreciate each moment as a gift and see a positive future. I must do this. God has given me the opportunity to love again and I don't want to waste it.

I woke up to Grandma Judy saying goodbye. I had a few hours of restless sleep, but sleep.

Matt helped me get ready for bed. Tomorrow would be a new day. Outpatient rehabilitation. Meeting with the therapist, going over a new game plan. All four of us would go.

It was 9:00 p.m. and Matt tucked me in. He had work to do.

Trying to navigate all this, my heart hurt for my husband. It reminded me of Matt's words to me: "Love is a verb." It's not a feeling; marriage isn't a ring worn, or a paper signed. It is not something endured but savored. It is the union of two people who have committed to each that they would sacrifice for the other's happiness and well-being. Marriage is something so beautiful and fearful all wrapped up in one. Marriage is a blessing, a commitment to be there for each other in sickness and in health. Sickness. How would I ever overcome this heartache for my husband? My love. My rock.

Chapter 15

Nightmares

I could not see what the future held, what tomorrow would bring. For now, I was fearful to close my eyes, to fall asleep, fearful of not waking up.

The nightmares persisted. As much as I tried to fight the demons that would torment me in my sleep, the pain, the fear, came out in the form of a silent scream. The beads of water started falling one after another, without a sign of stopping. *Scream let them know you are here*. But I couldn't move. I was frozen. The only thing that told me I was alive was the violent movement of my left side.

The muffled sounds of Matt's soothing words: "Come back to me," turned my world into a blur of reality. His painful expression slammed against me when I was called back to reality, trying desperately to escape the feeling of being lost in the unknown. The wilderness. The darkness of nothingness, the oblivion of unconsciousness.

Am I safe? I opened my eyes, frantically trying to find Matt in the dim light, listening to his voice. As I lay there, frozen guilt washed over me. How much more could he handle? I longed for Mary, my nighttime nurse, to visit me, feeling guilty that my love had to endure another sleepless night.

Matt tried to sing to me, to provide comfort, but his voice quivered, and I felt the salty tears roll down his face onto mine.

Chapter 16

Matt

A memory of that night... 3:30 in the morning and MK is thrashing again, trying desperately to fight the demons that invade her dreams. I turn on a dim light and find her eyes are open. Tears of panic are flooding in like water from a broken dam; she's drowning in fear. I know it. I continually repeat, "Come back to me, I'm right here," until her breathing stabilizes. She is desperately trying to find me in the darkness. I kiss her face and repeat "I love you."

Another night of horrific dreams. What is happening to my bright, beautiful girl? My heart hurts for her, but this cannot be about me. Now it's my turn for tears; I could not suppress them any longer. They splash on her face and I hold her, desperately holding on to what used to be. Mourning the loss of who she was; not wanting to face, not wanting to grasp the reality of what is coming. I try to sing to her, but I cannot sing the words that would provide comfort.

Neither one of us is getting enough sleep. I am no good to my wife or my family. I am exhausted, mentally and physically. I must find a way, I must make this work, I must be the husband to my Mary and the father to our girls while managing our home, Mary's care schedule, and work.

Our morning routine would be forever changing. I had to be flexible; I had to be strong.

Chapter 17
New Day, New Chance

I could tell it was morning; Matt and the girls were in the kitchen preparing breakfast. I looked over at the clock and it read 6:13 a.m.

Another restless night, my left side still letting me know she was here. I had to come up with a name for this uncontrollable muscle movement since it appears this was who I was right now. I had an unwanted companion.

Matt came in with a bright smile and the most amazing eyes. Not one feature makes Matt so handsome, though his eyes come close. People often speak of the color of eyes, as if that were of importance, yet he would be beautiful in any shade. From them came an intensity, honesty, gentleness. I knew he had not given up on finding solutions. This honest man, whom I loved, had shown no weakness but was incredible with finding strength, solutions. What he is, what is beautiful about him, came from deep within. How did I become so blessed with a husband who looks past my flaws and loves me for who I am, for what I have become? He gave me the strength I never thought I possessed.

"Good morning, sunshine," Matt sang to me. I gleefully smiled. He helped me up from the bed and escorted me to the bathroom. He helped me undress, then turned on the water in the shower. Today was day three of a new chance, a new life starting at home.

The shower was a walk-in. A small step up and over the rim and he sat me down on a shower chair that he had installed for my use. We were in there together. Matt was undressed. His beauty. His presence. I wondered when the last time was that we had taken a shower together. The passion that once was a key piece of our relationship is now like this water. It's warm. He was there for a purpose. The purpose was to help me with shampooing my hair, cleaning my body.

As I sat in the chair, Matt went behind me. Making sure the water was cascading over the top of my head. "Relax, I've got this, sweetie." My mind was in a state of relaxation as thousands of lukewarm drops darkened my hair and trickled over my face and down my back. Matt used vanilla shampoo and soap, something mild for my senses. He began massaging my scalp. His hands were so strong; his voice was my everything. My eyes closed and I let the warmth of his physical touch remind me I was loved, I was alive.

He helped me stand and step out of the shower. He wrapped a warm towel around my head and my body and sat me down in a chair he had placed in our closet. He then hopped back in the shower to get ready for the day.

His shower was fast. He didn't enjoy leaving me alone, waiting.

He quickly got dressed and helped me with a baggy sweatshirt and pants. No bra yet. The bruises from CPR over forty days ago were still healing. He made a mental note to speak with my doctor.

A quiet knock on the door; Aubrey happily said, "Dad, can I help Mom with her hair?"

"Yes, that would be a great help," Matt said.

We had an appointment at 8:30 with outpatient rehab and Matt had to check in with work. First day of reality.

Matt moved the chair from the closet to in front of my bathroom sink. Aubrey grabbed my hairbrush and a blow dryer. She smiled at me and said, "Mom, you smell so good. Do you like your new shampoo and soap?"

I smiled and nodded my head yes.

Aubrey bent down and said, "I'm so glad you are here."

I stared in the mirror. I didn't recognize this face. This person looked weary; she was tired. My left side was untamable. My hair had not been of any importance while I was in the hospital for forty days, tangled, broken and a mousey dull brown. My face said it all: I had stopped caring about my appearance sometime in my life, but when? I wondered. The state of my hair brought curiosity. Who was I before? Did my family always love me? We can assume a lot by appearances. My appearance. What should have been a glossy reddish-brown cut and color was a brittle and dull rats' nest.

Aubrey did her very best. After a blow-dry, she arranged it in a messy bun. That would work!

I smiled, and she kissed me on my forehead.

She helped me stand and attached my gait belt, reached for the walker and encouragingly said, "We've got today Mom, you will do great!"

We walked from the bath to the breakfast table. With her left hand, she grasped my gait belt and with her right she guided me. She reminded me to lift my feet, and we made our way to the delicious smells coming from the kitchen. Emily had been busy making sure the colors and textures were just right. She proudly placed my breakfast in front of me. "Good morning, Mama. You look great and smell delightful!" She kissed me on my forehead and asked how everything looked.

I smiled and nodded my head.

The four of us sat down and Matt went over the game plan for the day. Each of us had an important role to play. Outpatient rehab was not only for me but for the family. We would all have tasks to take on. Matt assured us that the game plan would be forever evolving depending upon what I could do and what I could tolerate.

"Girls, if you have questions for the therapist or your mom's doctor, be sure to write them down so we can make sure we address them. For instance, I have three on my list right now."

"Three, already, what are they, Dad?" Emily asked.

"Good question, Em."

Matt looked at me for approval. I was eager to see what he had written. So, I smiled and nodded my head yes. Matt began listing his questions.

"Your mom's sleep. Sleep is an important part of healing and your mom's left side gets worse at night, plus she is having night terrors. The bruising around her torso. It's very sensitive. The involuntary muscle movement on your mom's left side. I think one and three are related. If we can relax the involuntary muscle movement, I think she can get some rest."

I must have looked amused, because all three of them were staring at me, smiling.

Aubrey said, "Mom, you are here, and we know you comprehend what is going on. This will help all of us. Don't worry, we got you!"

"If you have anything else that needs to be addressed today, let's go over it; but for now, we need to load Mom in the car and drive to rehab," Matt said encouragingly.

Matt helped me with my coat, a bright pink, synthetic wool, mid-length style with four huge black shiny buttons. He kissed me on my left cheek and said: "You look like you are ready to conquer the day!"

I smiled and whispered, "We. Got. This!"

Chapter 18
Outpatient Rehab

My second car ride. Everyone was busy helping make this a successful outing. They carefully placed me in the passenger seat and Aubrey buckled me in with the seatbelt strap securing my left side. Emily folded up my walker and placed it in the car's trunk. Matt made sure I had all the paperwork and his notebook.

"Ready Spaghetti," Matt said as he held the driver's side door open for the girls to pile in. We only had a two-door Honda Civic that was low enough for me to get in and out of with the help of family.

There was something so familiar, so safe about this passenger seat. *The seat is cloth, not leather. Why did I think it was leather?* Is it because of the leather recliner that slowed down the blood clot that gave my family those few precious moments that saved my life? For now, I could only enjoy the safety, the quiet. My thoughts were quiet. Is this a magical car? I felt safe. I haven't felt safe in so long. And it's quiet! I didn't have to try, all I had to do was sit and take it all in.

We pulled out of the garage and were now on the road, a drive across town to Penrose Outpatient Rehabilitation.

I looked out the passenger window. The sun was tucked away behind gray, black, and white clouds which hung low over the city. Another sunless day. It looked like the sun had given up on trying to break through this curtain of clouds. It reflected my emotions. Gray. Everything seemed dark and dreary. I wanted it to be sunny again, to have the warmth of the sunlight splash on my face. To feel happy, to be carefree. Was it selfish, I wondered, to have such a desire, when I had been given the gift to live again, to love?

Matt made sure the car ride was quiet, so it didn't overstimulate the start of my day. Aubrey and Emily both fell asleep, which was a nice change. I loved hearing the girls in the back seat, near me. They, the three of them, would be my sunshine, my warmth, my life.

We drove around the parking lot for several minutes. Matt would pick up a handicap placard later today, for now, we had to use a handicap spot for unloading me and my walker. The girls woke up and began to giggle at the drool collected around their chins and over their coats. I never thought slobbering would be so funny, or did I? This brought a smile to my face. The real-life antics of my tribe.

Matt let the girls out of the back of the car and unlatched the trunk. Emily retrieved my walker, as Aubrey and Matt assisted me out of the car. I tried to stay calm as my eyes met Aubrey's. I reached for her, pleading with her not to let go of me, not to leave me. She smiled sweetly and said, "We've got this Mom; we are all in this together." I felt numb as tears gathered behind my eyes. Why was I

so afraid, what was I afraid of? I
couldn't understand.

Chapter 19
Outpatient Rehab Staff

Case Manager

They connected the outpatient rehabilitation center to Penrose Hospital. I had just left the inpatient rehabilitation a few days ago. Was I worried that they might readmit me? Was it because I just didn't know what to expect?

Emily grabbed my gait belt and Aubrey walked ahead. Off we went into the facility, moving at a snail's pace. Scared. Emily, so very encouraging, reminded me to lift my feet as we walked "one foot in front of the other." The walker had wheels; I relied heavily on the security it provided me. We scooted through the large automatic doors and Emily found me a seat as she surveyed the rehabilitation center.

Matt introduced himself to the kind person behind the front desk. She handed him a lot of paperwork that required my attention. Matt took a seat next to me and started going over the documents. One look at my confusion, and he gently kissed me on my forehead and quietly said, "You don't have to worry about this, love, you just focus on you for now."

Matt signed his name as my caretaker.

They called us back to a meeting room.

No windows, no natural light. The room was every shade of gray, from washed-out walls to a busy steel-blue desk. Every line was straight, every corner sharp, and the chairs looked as comfortable as what you would find in a dentist's office lobby. Nothing personal, no paintings on the walls, no pictures on the desk. The office was cold. Or was that just my mood? I wondered if how I felt was transferring to my surroundings, or were my surroundings reflecting my mood?

I moved forward, keeping my mind on my steps. My hands were becoming drenched in sweat; the taste of fear was tangible. Aubrey helped me sit down on the far-left seat. She stood behind me and forcefully placed her left hand on my left shoulder. This simple gesture helped my left side relax a little. I cradled my left arm, hoping this day would be over soon. Matt and Emily grabbed the other two open seats. I looked at Matt and he smiled confidently at me.

Files and files on the desk. Mine was in the front and center. It surprised me at how thin it seemed compared to the rest of the files cluttering the workspace.

My case manager briskly made her way into the room and sat behind her desk. She smiled sweetly at me, Matt, and the girls. "Your case is very fascinating. How are you feeling?" She asked slowly and carefully, enunciating each syllable.

I smiled and nodded my head.

"My name is Ms. Smith; I will be your case manager."

I smiled and nodded my head.

Ms. Smith was a tall, slender woman. She had short jet-black hair, golden brown eyes set far apart, beautiful olive skin, and a smile that could warm up the coldest days. I liked her already. When she spoke, she directed her comments towards me. I wasn't invisible.

I gave a deep sigh. A sigh of relief.

"I have been going over all your charts," She pointed at all the files on her desk. "You've had an extraordinary experience. I am happy to be on this journey with you and your family. I understand it's been a trying time for all of you." She looked lovingly at my family. "After talking to inpatient rehab and the doctors, we all feel you can make a significant improvement."

Matt asked, "Do you have a time frame when she can look forward to some independence, like driving or going back to work?"

Ms. Smith gave my husband a warm, empathetic smile and sweetly said, "Nothing is impossible. Mary, how are you feeling? I am sure this is all overwhelming, but we are here to help you find a new normal. All the specialists have spent many hours developing a game plan for your continued recovery."

"A game plan." I smiled and nodded my head.

Matt cautiously said, "You said a new normal!"

Ms. Smith smiled and said, "Yes, a new normal. Your wife's brain is damaged, and we will work alongside you to help her navigate. Mary, your specialists are eager to get started. Are you ready?"

I nodded my head mournfully. I could not imagine my life remaining this way. I didn't want to.

Ms. Smith said, "Mr. Podschweit, we will help you apply for long-term disability and Social Security. That process takes a while. Have you received the letter for a handicap parking pass?"

I zoned out. What was happening? I had to be more aware.

As Aubrey helped me up from the chair, Emily raced over to grab my walker. Matt and Ms. Smith continued with a brief conversation.

Ms. Smith stood from behind her desk and walked over to the door. She looked at me and stated, "Your schedule will never change while you are here. You will spend a half-hour with each therapist. Speech, physical, and occupational therapy three times a week, starting today. Once again, the format will never change."

Okay, speech therapy first. The most challenging of the three. They escorted me out of Ms. Smith's office down a bright hallway to speech therapy.

The hallway had the same personality as Ms. Smith's office. The floor was slate gray, but the walls were warm cream. Above, they made the ceiling from those polystyrene squares laid on a grid-like frame with fluorescent lights encased in the ceiling squares. I found the light abrasive. Difficult to focus. There were no pictures on the wall, no life, I guessed I should find comfort in that, but I didn't understand why. Above the only door in this long hallway was a sign that read "Speech." Aubrey knocked on the door and we heard a very calm voice say, "Come in!"

Aubrey opened the door, and the connection was instant.

Chapter 20
Speech Therapy

Katie stood to help me. She had set up five chairs around a circular table. Her office was windowless. Fluorescent light gave the appearance of daylight, but it wasn't real. It was a windowless space. They painted the office in a warm beige. On her gray desk sat a desktop computer, a notebook lying open, and a stack of files. A bookshelf bursting with books was in a corner, with yet another stack of papers under a paperweight that was shaped to look like a brain. To soundproof her office, she had a noise-canceling device running on a stand close to the door. A few pens were lying on a notepad in front of one chair. On her walls were posters of the alphabet, simple words, and a graphic of a voice box. There was nothing personal to be found anywhere. Katie was beautiful, with short curly blonde hair held back by the glasses she wore on top of her head. She stood a little over five feet. She had fair skin with pale blue kind eyes. Simple. No makeup, no frills. She was immediately welcoming, and I was happy about that. I didn't know what I was so afraid of. Once we were all seated at the table, she asked my family to introduce themselves as she scribbled on a sheet of paper in her notebook. She then began asking our daughters their ages and where they live.

After she finished gathering information, she turned to me and gave me a very gentle smile. "Mary, you have been through a lot, but you have also overcome a lot. I know it will seem overwhelming, but I need you to stay focused. We don't have a lot of time to spare, so let's get started.

Katie said, "Can you tell me your full name?"

"Yes," I said.

"Can you please tell me your name now?" she kindly asked.

"Mary (pause) Kaye (pause) Podschweit," I said in a hoarse, monotone whisper.

"Do you know what year it is?"

I nodded my head yes.

Katie smiled sweetly, "Can you please tell me?"

"19 (pause) 26," I said.

"Do you know the people in this room?"

I smiled and nodded my head again.

"Can you tell me?" Katie asked.

I nodded my head, not understanding what she wanted.

She smiled and wrote something down.

"Do you know what day it is?" Katie asked.

"Yes," I smiled.

"Can you tell me?"

"Yes," I nodded my head.

Katie began writing.

She held up letters of the alphabet, cards for children, and asked if I could read them.

I said, "Yes."

Katie smiled and asked, "Can you read them out loud?"

"Yes," I said with a puzzled look.

She gave me a very kind smile. She then said, "Do you want some homework?"

I nodded my head and said, "Yes."

Half an hour of questions and answers leave me exhausted. But we have more therapy sessions to go.

Speech therapy was a painful process.

Katie stood up and came out from behind the table. She gently said, "Physical therapy is waiting for you now." She asked the girls to help me to the room and asked if Matt had questions. He stayed back and the three of us made our way to PT.

Chapter 21
Physical Therapy

Everything was open. There wasn't a barrier between physical therapy (PT) and occupational therapy (OT). Natural sunlight would have filled this room if it weren't for the dismal morning. This room was too busy with other patients and therapists. My ears began shutting down. My senses were on overload. The smell of hand sanitizer, sweat, and fresh coffee and pastries that just came out of the oven over at OT overwhelmed me. *Is it going to be like this forever?* I hated this. The room began spinning and Aubrey hurriedly brought a seat over for me. *How did she know?* I wondered. She sat me down in the middle of the chaos. There was too much busy-ness, too much.

This room was in the open space of a large room. It had a bed to practice getting into and out of on your own, light weights, a bicycle, a wide balance beam, and parallel bars. Lots of different-sized balls, a light game on the wall to measure reaction time, and all kinds of torture devices.

Across the way along the west wall was a mock kitchen. That's where the bouquet of different scents was coming from. I'm sure on any other day I would have appreciated the aromas drifting in the air. But today, this morning, it was too much.

Many therapists were busy helping with other patients. All the activity was difficult to follow.

Randie came over to us. "You must be Mary!" she said with a beautiful bird-like chirp. Randie was an athlete, you could tell by how she carried herself. She was confident, with a strong medium build, short brown hair, and dark eyes. It reddened her skin from being outside. *I bet she's a runner*, I thought to myself.

I smiled and nodded my head, "Yes."

"Well, well, you've had quite the past two months."'

117

I looked down at my feet. *Two months. Two months. Come on brain, please remember.*

"Mary, are you okay?" Randie asked, not missing a beat.

I looked up at her, scared.

"It's very normal to feel overwhelmed in new environments. We will go at a pace we all are comfortable with. I think once we begin you will block everything else out."

Randie continued to explain to Aubrey and Emily that this was a very normal reaction.

"Are you ready to work on walking on your own?" she said with a smile.

"Walking?" I looked up at her, holding back the tears, and asked her, "Without (pause) the (pause) walker?" I whispered.

"Yes! I think we can get there; you need to believe you can. It will be a difficult task but as much as you have already overcome, I think I am looking at a living miracle."

I smiled and nodded my head.

"First, let's see where we need to begin. I can then have a better idea of where we need to start. Are you ready?"

I nodded my head.

Torture! That's what this was. I failed every test: sitting from the edge of the bed to stand on my own. Failed. Walking ten steps with the walker and without stopping. Failed. Bending over. Failed. Sitting in a chair unassisted. Failed. Throwing a ball. Failed. Failed. Failed.

Randie said optimistically, "Not bad for your first time. Would you like some homework?"

Not bad? Who is she talking to? I wondered

"Yes," I nodded my head, feeling defeated.

119

"Okay, Aubrey and Emily, we have to make sure your mom is walking every day. I will show you how to walk with her to make sure she is using her muscles and her brain." The girls each took turns with holding onto my gait belt as I hung on dearly to the walker.

Matt came out of the room with Katie and my case manager, Ms. Smith. When did she go into the room, I wondered? His eyes were dying, consumed with fear and great concern. We made eye contact, and he put on a sad empathetic smile, if that is even possible.

Chapter 22
Occupational Therapy

My therapist's name was Amber. Amber was in her early sixties. She had a stern appearance. She wore her gray hair tight around her face while her eyeglasses hung around her neck. The strap appeared new, a sign of pride: it's beaded. In a trance, I couldn't break the spell of trying to count the beads. *One, two, three, siven, wait, that's not a number. Come on, brain.* The beads were multi-colored. Red was my favorite, no blue... actually, all of it. It had a certain sparkle that kept my attention.

Amber introduced herself to my family. I looked up. We were all seated. What I remember most was her shade of lipstick, a shocking red which made her smile perfect. *I bet she loves colorful things. She was shaped like an orange. Orange. What a pleasant color. Orange. Oh boy, I would love an orange. Come on brain, focus.*

As we all sat at the table, Amber started going over the game plan with my family and me. Already mentally exhausted I began to shut down.

She tested my coordination by having  me pull out colored plugs and then try to put them back in the correct holes.

I was having a difficult time trying to focus. It was all too much. She took notes and put the game aside.

I would react whenever I heard laughter. They were telling stories about me in the kitchen. I sat, smiling and wondering: *was it really that bad*?

Suddenly, like flipping a switch on the wall, I began laughing. So unexpectedly. Laughter! I couldn't stop. I didn't understand why I was laughing. I looked at my family in panic, but the laughter kept going. I didn't know why I laughed so hard and suddenly. My breath came in quick gasps between the hilarity. I started to panic. What was going on? Tears gathered and started racing down my face. I pleaded with an apologetic mask, *forgive me. Forgive me.*

My family, who began laughing because they thought I was happy, quickly realized something else was happening. Emily held my arm and said, "Mom, are you okay?"

Amber intervened quickly. "Is this the first time she has exhibited spontaneous laughter or crying?"

Matt spoke in a hurry while he was coming over to reassure me, I would be okay. "Yes, please tell me this is part of the process!"

Matt came over alongside me, as Emily made room for him. He gently caressed my face and kissed my tear-stained face. He leaned in and whispered in my ear, "You're okay love, you're okay. Mary, honey, breathe with me. In and out. Deep breath in and blow out. Let's do that again."

Amber, rather proudly, said, "These responses are very common with brain injuries. Mary has limited control over her emotions. I recommend you let her emote. Allow her to feel. I understand your first instinct is to coddle but if she is in no danger, allow her to be overdramatic."

"Overdramatic!" I thought that was a terrible thing to say. "Overdramatic," as though I have a choice right now. I was not a child.

Matt looked over at the girls. Everyone was taken aback by what just happened and what was said.

A few minutes went by and I was back in control of my emotions.

Matt sat next to me, holding my right hand, which was grasping my left arm, which was really going to town now. Moving uncontrollably. Matt began breathing, allowing me to follow along.

Amber looked nonplussed about the time this has taken. Back to business with this one. I was sure at one time she was empathic. Perhaps it was just a bad day. I hoped so.

"Okay, let's get this session going again, shall we? Mary should not be in the kitchen." Amber said with a stern look on her face.

This time I genuinely chuckled at the thought of me in the kitchen. The good news for me was that I wasn't allowed. I could not be around sharp objects, not even a knife for use of dining. I could use nothing hot: not a hot stove, nor the microwave, not even a coffee pot.

"You will see there are many things that could be very dangerous for her in the kitchen." Amber was smug at this point. "I also want one of you to turn the shower on. Make sure it's the right temperature. I've seen too many patients with brain injuries burn themselves in the shower with hot water." She looked straight at my family, "Are we in agreement?"

My family sat quietly, and Matt finally said, "Yes, we can, and will all agree."

After all the warnings to my family, she then went into what I could work on.

"What I have in our notes is that Mary is yet to take care of herself. Does she use all of you to help with personal hygiene?" Amber asked.

"Yes, we all help her," Aubrey said, a bit defeated.

"Well, enough of that. She needs to be doing some of these things on her own. I am confident she will figure it out."

"How do you expect her to do anything without help!" Emily spoke up. She didn't like how Amber was talking down to me.

Amber looked amused. "She will figure it out. Listen, we are running out of time. I want to go over Mary's homework before you need to leave."

"Home (pause) work," I repeated softly and sighed.

My homework seemed simple, but I had yet to do any of this ... yet! Brush your own hair. Brush your teeth. Shower on your own. For all these things I have relied on others to help me; now I had to find a way. I would find a way. After all this time, to think I could do something on my own was overwhelming. I smiled and said "YES!" so clearly that it took everyone aback.

Matt had the biggest grin on his face and leaned over and kissed my forehead.

Amber stood up from the table and addressed the next patient, "I'll be right with you, just finishing up."

Matt and Emily stood up to help me get out of the chair. Aubrey raced for my walker. Matt grabbed my gait belt and said, "Let's go, honey!" with a huge grin.

When it was time to leave, they escorted me to a seat in the lobby and Matt with the girls made the rest of the appointments for me. Three times a week, every week for the month of January.

Aubrey came over and said, "You did great, Mom!"

I looked at her, confused. There's no way anyone would ever think I did a great job, except through the love and encouragement of my family. I vowed to myself, right then, that I would work. Even if I felt like giving up, I would push through.

Emily and Matt came over with a quick step and said, "Let's go get some coffee!"

Chapter 23

First Outing

Starbucks was on the way home.

Matt ran out to get the car, and the girls bundled me up in my hot pink coat with the large shiny black buttons. They attached the gait belt on the outside of my coat and out the door we went. I deliberately picked up my feet with the use of my trusty walker, this time with a sense of urgency.

The handicapped spot was open, so Matt pulled in, unlatched the trunk, and assisted me into the passenger seat. Aubrey folded up the walker as Emily climbed into the back seat.

Once we were all in the car, off we went in pursuit of hot coffee. I felt a family meeting was coming, and I thought about what I wanted to say all the way there. I had to tell them; I had to convince them of what? *Come on brain, you had it a few minutes ago, what was it you want to say?*

131

Starbucks. I hadn't had one in so long. Matt said, "Sweetie, do you want your regular?"

Confusion danced across my face and Matt smiled. "Don't worry honey, I can help you."

Aubrey sat with me in the warmth of the coffee shop. The air smelled delicious. All the aromas swirling with everything good. The freshly brewed coffee, pastries, the cozy atmosphere, the soft music in the background. We were tucked away near the back at a comfortable corner table. The floor to ceiling windows would show Pikes Peak, but today the heavy air was preventing us from seeing the beauty of Colorado Springs. I sat and stared, taking it all in. I examined every feature of Aubrey. Her head was down, and she was texting her friends—undoubtedly with updates about rehab this morning. I love her. Her beauty shines from within. Her sweet spirit, full of love, full of life.

I accidentally made eye contact with the only other customers, a couple who stopped reading their newspapers to provide an empathetic smile. I could tell they were talking about me. I looked away. How was I to respond to strangers being kind? I didn't know, so I continued looking around the coffee shop. Matt and I made eye contact and his smile was all I needed. His smile was of pride, was of love, was of a gentle spirit unlike any other. I had never been to this coffee shop before, or at least I didn't remember being here, but it was a place I could sit in for hours and listen to my family.

We would be okay.

Matt and Emily came over with fresh pastries. Coffee would be on its way soon. Matt snuggled next to me and whispered, "You showed everyone today that you will not settle. Honey, I need you to never give up. Some days will be hard, but I believe in you. I need you to believe."

133

Aubrey went to retrieve our coffee, and we all sat down for our family meeting.

"While the girls worked with you, honey, I spoke to Katie and your case manager, Ms. Smith, privately. I don't want to worry you. All I want to say is I am so proud of you. You tried. You communicated on your own. I can tell you are displeased, and I want you to hang on to this feeling. If you can find the competitive spirit you once had, you will fight to win this battle." Matt began sharing about his conversations. Most of his questions had been answered. He would go with me to see my doctor the next day.

I zoned out in my own thoughts, trying to remember what had happened in therapy.

Matt grabbed for my hand. "I think—actually, I know—we can do this, especially watching you today. You did better than anyone had planned."

Chapter 24
Family Decisions

"I have to go back to work. I need to at least appear in the office," Matt said.

Oh, my goodness, this is delicious. What is it? I wondered to myself. Taking sips of hot coffee, I lost my concentration again.

"Mom," Aubrey said, "Emily, and I have been talking and I have decided to stay at home to help you. Emily has to leave for school in a few days."

"We believe in you and are so encouraged with your ability to try, Mom. It's amazing to see you work so hard." Emily shared her stories of the past 45 days. I tried to listen, to comprehend, but once again I was lost in the nothingness that was consuming me.

I must ask what kind of coffee this is. Has this always been my favorite? If so, I have good taste! I smiled to myself.

"There she is!" Matt exclaimed, "There's that smile!"

We sat in the coffee shop going over today's schedule. I tuned out and was sleepy. My left side began to act out. Aubrey noticed that I was hugging my left arm.

"Mom is tired," Aubrey said so caringly, "We should get home."

My next memory was of Matt slipping into our bedroom, leaning over the bed, and telling me he would see me in a few hours. He needed to stop by the office but reassured me the girls were there if I needed anything.

Worry consumed me at that moment. Things I felt, I fear, consumed me. He couldn't leave. What would we do if he was hurt? Everything I should have done the day I was injured, November 21, 2013, coupled with all my perceived failures, dominated my mind. I thought about Matt's actions and words, finding them comforting. My hero. I couldn't lose him. Festering guilt and this short-term memory loss rendered my mind ineffective. Lost, I am lost, scared and confused. I struggled with words.

"Honey, I will be only a phone call away. I will be gone for just a few hours. I have to go, but I will return." Matt smiled warmly. He wanted to help me communicate but knew I had to figure it out, find the words. He leaned over and kissed my tears.

I lay there dwelling on the minute details of this new life. The big picture escaped me at that moment. I had no opportunity to be my old self; I was losing the person I used to be. I was falling backward with nothing to hang on to. Nothing to grab. Nothing to break this fall. I closed my eyes and fell asleep with the anguish of my life now.

Chapter 25
Despair

Depression. "What ifs" plagued me. All I could do at that moment was hide in despair. Depression. My mind plummeted downward into less and less light, and darkness beyond measure. The gray day turned black. The songbirds outside my window stopped singing. It seemed like everything around me had taken on this dullness.

Is there a bottom to the mind's pain? Is there any branch of hope, or something to catch or hold on to? Is there some rescuing idea that can come from my thoughts? How much darkness can one take with no light? I fell deeper into the despair that the doctors had warned us about.

So, this was normal? This was awful. I hated this. I couldn't find hope, joy, or love from within, so it had to enter from outside. If I could pray to give this to HIM, to turn these thoughts of despair toward the Almighty One, even for a flashing moment, then that would be a moment of relief. Why? What lesson is to be learned in this moment? He sent an angel to me while in rehabilitation. While I was in ICU, HE never left me, but now I felt so alone, so scared.

I had to find the light, no matter how big or how small. HIS light is warm and would brighten the dark and scary thoughts that were swallowing me. HIS light is love and hope and joy. Even a glimmer would give me what I needed at this moment of truth. I had chosen to live for Matt, our daughters, and HIM. HE has not left me; HIS power is greater than this... this... I didn't even know what to call it. In this downward plunge, falling, falling, unable to scream, unable to save me, HE reached for me. HE stopped me from drowning in a bottomless pit of gloom. HIS light was only a spark, but it was here.

I woke to Matt kissing me on my drenched face. "Hey, sleepyhead! Another bad dream?"

Matt's strong hand caressed my face just as HIS strong hand reached and caught me. He pulled me up and cradled me in his arms. He whispered, "Breathe."

I lay confused about what had happened. Matt sensed this and explained that he has been gone for a few hours. He called home, and the girls said I was still in bed, probably exhausted from rehab. "You are safe now, honey. You are safe."

The aroma coming from the kitchen made my stomach rumble. I had slept through lunch. The girls had called their dad and asked if they should wake me, but the consensus was that if I was asleep, let me sleep. I could eat when I was awake, but rest would be an important part of healing.

Matt helped me to my feet and escorted me into the dining room. He slid my chair in and I was immediately served an enormous platter of food: an omelet with ham and vegetables so finely chopped you could not see them, fried potatoes, and fresh bananas and cantaloupe. Plus, there was a chilled glass of whole milk and a basket of freshly baked rolls with real butter.

I brought a fresh, warm roll to my nose and inhaled deeply. It smelled rich, promising a delightful taste. I picked up a knife, then startled myself by dropping it on my plate, "clang", it echoed throughout the room. Everyone just sat and stared with huge grins on their faces. The surprise on Matt's face brought an embarrassed smile to mine.

Matt said, "I can do that for you, sweetie." He applied a generous helping of thick, creamy yellow butter. My mouth was watering, longing to taste this delightful treat. I tried to rip off a chunk of bread but could not manage. The girls sat there, wide-eyed and happy. Matt tore a piece of bread into bite-sized pieces for me. With my right hand, I reached over my agitated left side and accepted the offering. Stuffing the piece of buttered bread into my mouth, I savored the soft, warm, sweet smell and taste. I enjoyed all the food prepared for us that evening. I appreciated every bite. Every sensation. Every giggle and every conversation.

After dinner, I asked if I could shower and go back to bed. Tomorrow would be another full day of appointments. One thing I had kept from today's torture sessions was that rest is the greatest healing factor. With the nightmares and my left side taking on a life of its own, any time spent resting would be a blessing. I would have to force it, force my body to relax.

Chapter 26
Love is a Verb

Matt said, "Honey, I can help you."

"Thank," I said in my soft, raspy monotone.

Eight o'clock p.m. and off we went with the walker and gait belt in tow. I lifted my feet intentionally as I scooted the walker. Matt had put a chair in our bathroom, so he assisted me in sitting down. He gestured with his hand and said, "Sweetie, give me a minute and I will join you."

"No. (pause) Need to (pause) do (sigh) this," I replied hopefully.

Matt leaned in to look at me. Curiosity made his beautiful, kind face glow. "Did you just say you want to try on your own?"

I smiled and nodded my head.

Matt smiled lovingly and said, "I'll help you in the shower and make sure you can reach the soap and shampoo. I'll sit here until you are ready."

I smiled.

"I am so proud of you." Matt said.

He turned on the shower before helping me stand and taking off my clothing. He guided me as I sat down in the shower, on the stool he had thoughtfully placed for my safety. He turned the water on high. I let it beat over my chest in a steamy continuous stream. Closing my eyes as the heat of the water soaked into my skin, I inhaled and held my breath, raised my head, and let the downfall of tears wash away the day.

While I was engrossed with the water cascading down my body and massaging my muscles, Matt began singing to me our song, *I'll Dream of You Again*.

I was not strong enough to pick up the shampoo bottle. I tapped on the shower door. Matt peeked in. He politely asked, "Do you need me to help you?"

I nodded my head in exasperation.

I bent my neck with my chin touching my chest. I closed my eyes and breathed through my mouth. The water ran over my head like a rain's sweet caress.

I tried to remember how I had fallen in love with this man. Some might say I was lucky, but I knew it blessed me to have him as my partner.

I lifted my head out of the stream of water. My hair is damp enough for Matt to shampoo. I let the water beat on my chest. Matt grabbed the shampoo bottle and asked if I was ready.

I nodded my head yes.

Slowly, I raised a hand and placed it over his as he shampooed my hair. I mouthed, "Thank you for loving me." He couldn't see my face or hear my whisper, but he leaned over and kissed my cheek.

After I was clean and dry, he put fresh pajamas on me and escorted me to our bedroom. He went to help me in bed, and I waved my hand. I wanted to try it on my own.

This tiny gesture brought my husband to his knees. Someday I would ask him what he went through while I was fighting for my life, fighting to stay. But tonight, I didn't think I could handle his answer.

His encouragement meant everything to me. His love is my glue, bonding my broken life together.

I wondered about true love. Is it you feel like the other person is the reason your life is beautiful even when it's broken? Is it being lost in his voice, his smile, his gentle eyes? These were the thoughts that kept me trying. To love. It's a verb, not an emotion. It's a choice. He loves me. I couldn't think of a better feeling, because when you feel low and you talk to them, all they say is, "It will be all right; I'm right here." These simple words were the light in the darkness, were the strong hand pulling me out of despair.

I could not get into bed by myself. I tried, truly I did. But with every attempt, just like in rehab, I failed.

Matt stood by, fighting the urge to help until I looked up at him and said, "Help me? Please!" with a bright smile.

I smiled. That's what Matt saw, my smile. He leaned over and encouragingly said, "Honey, you would not have attempted this last night, and now look at you. We will get through this together; I'll be right here for you always!"

He laid me down and tucked me in, keeping my feet exposed. He said I would always kick the covers off my feet while in the hospital. "It might provide some comfort for you. Let's see if it works tonight."

With me cradling my left arm and tucked into bed, it didn't take long for me to fall asleep. After a challenging day of rehab, a delicious dinner, and a hot shower, I was exhausted.

Matt kissed me on my head and said, "I'll be in bed soon, sweetie."

Chapter 27
Paralyzed with Fear

I tried to scream, but I couldn't move, I was tied down and gagged. I tried to reach out, but it paralyzed me, fear, fear immobilized me. "Matt, Matt! I am here. I am still here!" I was in the dark. Unable to speak, unable to move. Just falling. I kept falling into blackness. I saw a spark of light. Just a spark, not enough to see my way through this darkness. "Oh God, please help me! Please let me live!"

A strong hand pulled me towards the light and held me tightly, whispering, "I am here. I've got you!" I woke up. Tears were drowning me. Were they my tears or Matt's? He continued to hold me, whispering, "I've got you. I've got you!"

Chapter 28
3:30 a.m. Matt

A memory from that night... I awake to my Mary crying, frozen in fear. She's having another nightmare. My heart hurts. I wish I could take her place. Take whatever she is feeling and slaughter the cruel dreams she is having. Her left side is uncontrollable. She is not aware of her surroundings. She is panicked and in terror. All I can do is hold her and repeat "I've got you. I've got you!" A few minutes later she can open her eyes. Her heart is racing. Her breathing, short gasps. I kiss her eyes. My tears are flowing freely over hers. I continue to hold her and we both shed tears of pain, relief, hope, and fear. I truly don't understand what is going on or how to help I just know she needs me, and I will be here for her. I will be here. I lean in and wrap my arms around her, stilling her left side. I can imagine that left side reminding us "I'm still here!" in a wicked tone.

I whispered, "I'm sorry!"

How can she get better if every time she closes her eyes for some rest, she is fighting away the shock of what she has been through?

Mary falls half asleep while I am holding her.

Half asleep, half awake, fear is her companion. Unwanted, not invited companion. I close my eyes, but sleep will have to come at another time. Now, my wife needs me. I must be strong. I must help. I will speak to MK's doctor in a few hours.

Chapter 29
Day of Decisions

Matt kissed Emily on the cheek, "Good Morning, sweetie!"

"Good morning, Papa! Coach Rita says hello," Emily said sweetly.

Matt began making breakfast. Everything was creamy yellow. Eggs! Eggs would work.

"Emily, will you help Mom this morning while I make breakfast?"

Matt was unaware that Emily was still on the phone. She smiled and said, "Of course, Dad."

Emily hung up with her college coach and skipped into the bedroom.

"Good morning, beautiful!"

I smiled up at our youngest daughter.

"Are you ready to get up and get ready for your day, Mama?" Emily sang.

I smiled and nodded my head.

Emily assisted me to sit up and asked me if I wanted to stand on my own.

I smiled at her and nodded my head yes.

Emily put the walker in front of me and said, "Remember to use a walker for support. Hang on tight and move your body forward with momentum."

I tried and failed.

Emily, "It's okay. Let's try again."

I tried. Truly I did. I think most would have been sad about their failed attempt, but I had sunshine, the warmth, the glow of Emily to make me feel loved and I couldn't think of a better way to start the day.

"It's okay, Mom. Thank you for trying. I wouldn't be surprised if you had this down in a few days."

Emily helped me to the breakfast table. She slid my chair in as Matt put what would have been a delicious meal in front of me. I could only stare and look down with my right hand grasping my left arm. I needed orange. Matt saw my confusion and quickly realized what was happening. He said whimsically, "What's your color of the day, honey?"

I looked up at his inviting grin; how could I not smile back?

"Orange," I tried to say.

"Orange? That might be more difficult. Do you remember you can't have any citrus?" Matt asked gently, choosing his words carefully so as not to upset me.

I nodded my head, feeling forlorn.

"Looks like a challenge, Dad!" Emily exclaimed. "I'll see what we have that is orange."

Emily went into the kitchen and pulled out the sharp cheddar cheese. "Dad, let's melt this over her eggs until we can figure out what to do next."

Perfect, great solution. I would have to be flexible; although this wasn't what I wanted; it would have to do. Each of us was making sacrifices. I recognized how important it was to go along with the changes that had to be made, changes for me. It would be the only way for all of us to make this work.

Though my left side was moving, Matt could help me dress in sweatpants and a baggy sweatshirt. The bruises were very tender and hurt to touch. I didn't have to say anything; Matt knew, he sensed how uncomfortable I was when he helped me shower. He took the time to examine the injuries and make sure none of them felt hot. I winced but did not fight the examination.

After dressing me and helping me brush my teeth, he put my hair in a messy bun, then tenderly kissed me on top of my head. "Are you ready to meet your new doctor?" he asked.

He helped me to my feet and placed the walker in front of me. After putting on my pink coat with the shiny black buttons, then the gait belt, he said, "Emily, we will be back. Could you make a grocery list with orange foods for your mom?"

"Of course, Dad; can I help with Mom?"

Matt kindly said to her, "I've got this; your mom and I will be a few hours."

After gently placing me in the passenger seat, Matt put my walker in the car's trunk. He hopped in the driver's side and sighed, "Alone, just the two of us. It feels good."

I must have given him the biggest smile because he leaned over and kissed me right on the mouth.

This took me aback; I looked shocked. He jokingly said, "Are you ready, babe?"

"Babe?" I smiled.

Off we went. It was a very short drive to the doctors' office. Matt said in a hopeful way, "We will walk here someday, and as quickly as you are coming around, I suspect it will be sooner than later."

The sun was up, and it was a beautiful day. The clouds were a billowy white, like cotton balls. Yes, like cotton balls in the sky. I giggled at this thought. Spending time with Matt, alone, out of the house was exhilarating. He always makes me laugh! Always love.

We drove up to the doctors' office building. Matt swung the car through the drop-off. This was a circular drive with a covering over the drop-off and pick-up area. He put the car in park, unlatched the trunk and retrieved my walker. He enthusiastically opened my door and said, "Me lady" with a bow and helped me out. He then escorted me through the automatic doors towards a seat in the prestigious lobby, kissed me on my head, and said "I'll be right back!" Off he went. So happy, so upbeat, so mysterious!

Matt came back rather quickly. "Scored a great parking spot!"

He helped me to the elevator. We stepped inside. It's a wood panel box with safety bars. The building only had two floors and a basement! I wondered what was in the basement. Matt pushed the second-floor button. The doors slowly closed. Slowly. I looked at Matt and he is smiling. "I think we could try the stairs and it would be faster!" He was teasing me, wasn't he?

We stepped off the elevator into a huge lobby. With a puzzled look, a nurse said, "Mary Pod-schhhh-wit?"

Matt whispered to me, "That was quick!"

"Right here!" he raised his hand. The nurse looked over at us and gave us an empathetic smile.

Chapter 30

Dr. G

We made our way to the doctor's office. Not an exam room but her office. I looked up at Matt; he gave a small shrug and helped me sit down. The nurse entered the room without slowing her stride at all. One moment she was talking in the hallway—to the doctor, I presume—and the next moment she was grabbing my hand and finding a pulse. She opened a laptop and wrote something down. She opened a desk drawer and took out a blood pressure cuff. I began to tremble, like a kicked dog. Why, why was I scared? She looked at me and slowed down. "It's normal to be afraid, especially after everything you have been through. I need to do this, though. It's important to trace your vitals." She looked at Matt for reassurance.

Matt grabbed my hand. "Are you okay, sweetie?"

I nodded my head yes.

All my vitals taken; the nurse said the doctor would be in shortly. As quickly as she came in, she left. No friendly "How are you?"

I begged for Matt to hold me. I was shaking. Why was I shaking? I didn't know why, and I didn't know how to stop.

He reached over and brought me into the cradle of his arms. I closed my eyes as silent tears cascaded down my face.

Dr. G walked into the room. Matt went to stand, but after one look at me, she politely asked him to stay seated.

Dr. G was a silver-haired doctor which made her seem wise. Kind features, non-threatening. She stood about 5'7" with a medium build. Her lab coat was stark white. No makeup, no distinguishing features. Her movements were unhurried, deliberate. Her speech was direct. Great enunciation and diction. I wondered to myself if I used to notice these traits before. My mind wandered. When I looked over at Dr. G, I saw she was having a conversation with us, but had noticed that I had checked out. There appeared to be a warm light surrounding her. I closed my eyes, thinking it was the natural light giving her the glow.

Dr. G. said, "Gloria, close the blinds, please."

Gloria. That's the nurse's name. How long had she been here, I wondered?

"Is that better?" Dr. G. asked me.

I politely nodded my head. But the light was illuminating now, surrounding her. I wasn't afraid. It was a comfort. It was a brilliant yellow, no orange. *Come on, you know the colors.*

I looked at Matt and a warm pink light surrounded him. Pink!

I sat quietly, not wanting to say anything. Dr. G. was very sensitive. She asked us to her office in hopes it would be less threatening for me, which it was. Matt pulled out his notebook full of questions. Dr. G. smiled at him, grateful for his attention and care.

"I've gone over your charts and spoken to several doctors regarding your case. Mary, are you able to understand what I am saying?"

"Yes," I whispered.

"You've had quite the journey and are recovering; that says something about your tenacity and your family. Matt, let me address your questions."

Questions? How long was I zoned out? I wondered.

"I'm afraid I can't give Mary any medication that will help her sleep. She has two significant things going on in her cranium. One is the cerebral hypoxia which is hypoxia (reduced supply of oxygen), specifically involving the brain. When the brain is completely deprived of oxygen, it is called cerebral anoxia or anoxic brain injury. Mary has this from coding three times.

"The other is more complicated. We each have five dopamine receptors. Dopamine is a naturally occurring chemical in the body that functions as a neurotransmitter and neurohormone. It primarily affects movement control, emotions, and the pleasure and reward centers of the brain. It activates five dopamine receptors, D1 through D5, which are found throughout the brain and body."

Dr. G. was drawing a picture of a brain, my brain?

"We classify the receptors into either the D1-like receptor family or the D2-like receptor family, based upon morphological, pharmaceutical, and functional properties. Mary had a significant reaction to Haldol while in ICU. Although this drug is a typical antipsychotic medication. They use Haldol in the treatment of tics, delirium, agitation, acute psychosis, and hallucinations. Unfortunately, it came with risks. From the last brain scan, it shows that two, possibly three of Mary's dopamine receptors appear to be significantly damaged, which is causing her muscle stiffness and repetitive, involuntary muscle movements, or tics, as you can see. By reviewing her medical records, it's clear that she was showing signs of ICU delirium. With the damage done to her receptors, I have spoken to several doctors and we feel it's best to keep Mary on as few drugs as possible until the Haldol wears off.

But understand, we don't know if the damage is permanent. Another name for this involuntary muscle movement is Tardive Dyskinesia. There are no treatment options, but they have a drug that is being tested. But, as I've said earlier, I would not recommend any medication unless it's lifesaving. Until then, only time will tell how much is permanent damage and how much is temporary."

Matt shook his head, as though he understood what was being said.

"It appears Mary also has a mutation of the thrombomodulin gene, which is a genetic blood clotting disorder. It's important to have your daughters tested to rule out this gene. If they test positive, they will need to take some precautions with their own health. I recommend having this test done sooner than later."

Matt nodded his head. He was taking all this information in, being sure to write it down to discuss it with our daughters.

"The bruising is still very significant around her torso. You must monitor this, and if it ever feels warm to the touch DO NOT," Dr. G. said with some urgency, "hesitate. Go directly to the ER."

Matt looked up from taking notes. He did not look alarmed; he looked calm and reassuring. He nodded his head.

"As far as her sleep and the night terrors, it seems like you are doing everything you can. I am sorry she has these. Mary, please address this when you see a neurologist." She looked over at Matt, "You need to find time to rest Matt, otherwise, we might find you in my office."

"Matt, Matt can't get sick!" Panic must have masked my face.

Dr. G cautiously said, "He will take care of himself and you; no need for you to be concerned."

As Matt and Dr. G. were finishing up, I closed my eyes. I hated this. All of this.

Dr. G. said, "You will find yourself again, Mary. I know this is all overwhelming, but I believe in you. I want you to believe in yourself. When Gloria did the INR, test it came back at 1.9. We need this between 2.0 and 3.0, so we must adjust your Warfarin, Mary. Matt, do you keep track of her medicines?"

When did I have an INR test done? I looked down at my finger on my right hand and saw a bandage over my right index finger. I had to be more present.

"Yes, she is on blood pressure medicine and blood thinners, Tylenol as needed," Matt said calmly.

"I will see you next week. We are adjusting her dose of Warfarin and she will need this monitored."

An hour later, though it seemed like more, we left Dr. G's office. An hour with a doctor. An hour. *How thoughtful.*

Matt said, "I like her. Do you?"

I smiled and nodded my head.

Chapter 31
Tenderly

Matt made my appointments and off we went to the car. Once we were both buckled in, he began driving. "Beautiful morning, isn't it?" He smiled at me. "Let's go to the park; we can sit in the car and enjoy the scenery."

I smiled and whispered, "Okay, thank you!"

Matt leaned over and moved a small lock of hair that must have fallen from my bun. My pulse raced as he brushed the hair out of the way and with his other hand he reached for my hand. I looked into his eyes and saw deep pools of blue that displayed his soul. The pink aura around him shone brightly with glowing bolts of yellow. His lips touched my cheek. Time stopped. My heart came to a halt. My breath caught in my throat. Our fingers locked together like puzzle pieces. As the soft skin of his mouth left the side of my face, the exact spot where they had come into contact burned and tingled. A small grin crept onto my face and my cheeks painted themselves rose red. He pulled away silently, but our eyes locked, having a private conversation of their own. Love, love was winning this day.

Matt pulled up to a man-made pond on our way home. He parked the car so we could look out at the mountains. "Breathtaking!" he exclaimed.

I smiled and nodded my head and looked over at him. He wasn't looking at the mountains or their majestic reflection on the water, but me. He was talking about me! I began to blush. I felt the heat rise and redden my cheeks again. The blood seared my cheeks; for a minute I thought my face was on fire. Suddenly I felt awkward, demure, and shy; I even avoided eye contact.

Matt cupped my face in his slender hands and kissed me, gently, longingly. He whispered through tears, "We will be okay, no matter the outcome. I love you with every part of my soul, you are my reason to get up every day, you give me the courage to exist. The love we share trusts and has responsibilities, but not rights. I have no right to your heart, but I am blessed to love you with my own. I have no right to your time, but I am honored to share these moments. It is for me to do what is best for you; not to seek fulfillment of my own desires, but to make your well-being a priority. It is for me to seek what would make you happy, what brings a smile to your face, what refreshes your soul. When you hurt, I hurt too, how can I not? When you are scared and fighting these night terrors, I will be with you, love; we are in this together. I am proud to be yours and you mine."

I looked into his eyes, his eyes. Today Matt's eyes reflected the blue hue from... what? The mountains, the pond, the sky? Or perhaps a combination of all three? Today his eyes were blue, some days they were green, but today, today they were a life-giving blue. His eyes were a cloudless sky. His eyes were comfortable, warm, familiar, trusting. The pink hue surrounding him was radiant now. I smiled and felt secure, safe.

Chapter 32

Emily Leaves for College

"Sweetie, Emily has to leave for college tomorrow morning. She is going to Denver tonight to stay with Grandma Judy. It will be hard on her and on you. It scares her to leave you, no matter how much reassurance I give her. Do you understand?"

I had known this day would come. I wanted this for her. I wanted this for both our girls, to live their lives. Find their way. I said, "Yes, (pause) I'll be okay."

My words took aback Matt. "Oh Mary, you are, love! So unselfish, always a great mother to our girls. I know it will be hard, but we will all make this work, and perhaps we can go see Emily and watch her play sand volleyball. Coach Rita would love to see you. All of Emily's teammates and coaches have been very supportive. I think it's a good goal to have."

I must have looked surprised. The thought I could fly, walk, or enjoy watching volleyball made my eyes misty.

Matt smiled and said, "Shall we go back home now?"

We drove the short distance home. Matt sang a VeggieTales song along the way.

"If you like to talk to tomatoes,

If a squash can make you smile,

If you like to waltz with potatoes

Up and down the produce aisle,

Have we got a show for you!"

Someday I would sing with him; until then, I would cherish this time of listening, laughing, and living.

We arrived home to an empty house. Matt was concerned because he had to check in at the office. He began to make lunch for us while he was on the phone with his work. Just then Aubrey and Emily came home with vigor in their steps, laughing at an inside joke.

"Mom!" they both said in unison. They showered me with kisses.

After a few minutes of excitement, Aubrey charged downstairs and Emily looked at me, so pleased.

"Mom," Emily bent down and touched my right arm. "I got you something to help you along the way. I wish I could stay, but Dad said you understand, and you want me to go back to school. Is this right?"

"Yes," I said, holding back the tears.

"I know it seems basic, but I thought this could be helpful!" she said with a beautiful grin.

She handed me a children's book: *Green Eggs and Ham* by Dr. Seuss. The orange cover was captivating; the book was small enough for me to hold. The new book had a glossy cover and large print. I couldn't help myself, I had to look inside. Emily quickly

183

whispered, "You and Dad can read that later," she said with a wink.

"It was my favorite book, the first book I read out loud," Emily reminisced. "Remember all the time you spent helping me with sounds and words? I would curl up on your lap with this book and we would read it repeatedly. I want this to be your first book you can read out loud."

"*Green* (pause) *Eggs and Ham*," I said out loud, and then I smiled. Matt stopped what he was doing and turned to stare at me. I was blushing again.

"Mary, you are doing great! Look at you sweetie, you're glowing!" Matt said affectionately.

His pink light was dancing. And now the girls had a brilliant blue light encircling them. What was happening to my eyesight? I was afraid to say anything, so I continued to enjoy the auras.

Emily bounced downstairs as quickly as she came through the doors, off she went to finish packing.

Matt decided to work from home for a few weeks until we could set up a new schedule to help with all my care.

As I sat listening to the sounds of my family, I was curious. Did Emily feel sad about leaving a place so rich in love, a place where fond memories grew? Where the family was going through difficult changes, yet celebrate each day full of small victories? I knew that the strands of love would keep us together even when we were far apart. I had to be strong; I had to make the changes and the sacrifices necessary for her to leave confidently. I did not want Emily to question the decision to go back to school. I never wanted her to think of leaving meant she loved me less. I knew that it meant she loved me and believed we would all find a way out of this darkness.

As Emily was preparing to leave with her ride to Denver, she helped me to the living room and sat me down by the large window looking out over the evergreen trees. While she brushed my hair, she quietly said, "Mom, I will call you every day. I know you don't like to be on the phone, but I will need to hear your voice and listen to stories about your day. Promise me you will answer. Promise me, Mom. I don't think I can do this if I can't talk to you every day!"

"I promise." I didn't want to look at her; I didn't want to cry. I wanted her to see me as strong, but she stepped in front of me. The lights danced across her, each color slowly fading into another. The lights were beautiful, swaying and changing and illuminating the world, my world, my baby girl. Their glow, their shine, everything about them was beautiful. "That's what is so special about Emily. Her compassionate, empathic, and competitive spirit," I thought to myself. "I wonder why I have never noticed this light before." I looked up at her and smiled. "I promise!" I said with a more confident tone, "I promise!"

She leaned down and kissed me on my cheek. "I love you, Mom. Thanks for fighting to stay with us," she said as she put the hairbrush down on the side table and walked away.

Chapter 33
It's too Quiet

I heard Matt and Aubrey saying goodbye as they helped Emily with her luggage. I heard hugs and kisses; I heard whispers and sniffles, but I just stared outside at the evergreen trees, looking for the birds in the trees. I heard the door close, and I heard movement. But I continued to sit staring outside. I closed my heavy eyes and slept. I slept restlessly, hoping for a dreamless sleep. Suddenly, I was startled awake by the quiet.

Panicked by the quiet, I wondered, "Am I alone?"

My loneliness thrived until it dominated my emotions. I sat in the dark, quietly waiting for some noise, someone to come over. *Is this a dream or reality?* I wondered, trying to listen to my breathing. *Wait, am I breathing?* Panic set in.

I understand that some people revel in the sensory calm that isolation can bring, and the creativity that silence can bring to life. For me, being alone was a nightmare. It flooded me with "what ifs," my deepest fears clawed at the base of my throat and buried themselves in my chest, trying to find the quickening of my heart. Memories of inpatient rehab danced around the room, eclipsing the plague of darkness; time was blurred. I tried to escape, to call for help, then a white sheet covered my face. I tried to tell them, "I am here. I am here!" but no one listened. I tried to reach up, but they tied my hands down. No, no, no this couldn't be happening. This couldn't be. What was reality? Had I been in the hospital all this time? Was this hell?

I cried, "Jesus, don't leave me!" but I couldn't speak out loud. They gagged me; something was down my throat. I couldn't breathe. Tears flooded my face; I was drowning. Drowning in silent screams, in sweat, in the water that seemed to cascade from a broken dam. "Matt!" I tried to scream, but nothing came out. I coughed, trying to breathe before it completely covered me in water. I heard a splash. I couldn't see anything; I was too scared to open my eyes.

"Mary, Mary, wake up! WAKE UP!" I heard shouting. They must know I was alive; they must know I was still here. "Please, Jesus, please save me!" Someone grabbed me by the shoulders and held on tight. I collapsed into his arms and sobbed.

"I've got you now. I've got you." Matt was holding me, rocking me back and forth. He was trying desperately to calm me, to stop me from shaking. "I've got you," he whispered through tears of his own. His embrace was strong, capturing my left side like a cowboy wrestles steers. His strength reassured me I was alive.

My breathing became more in control as gasps of air filled my lungs. Matt felt me relax. He pushed me away to examine me, to make sure I didn't hurt myself.

"Another horrific dream?" he asked, already knowing the answer.

I could only nod as a gasp of breath forced my lungs to expand.

He reached for a box of tissues and began to gently wipe away the sweat and tears that have drenched my hairline, cheeks, and neck.

"I will listen if you want to talk about it," Matt said cautiously, looking at me to make sure I understood.

"I. Don't. Know. What to say." I whispered.

He smiled. I was communicating. That's a great sign.

After he was done cleaning my face, that messy representation of life and death, he lovingly kissed my forehead. He said, "You must be hungry. I've been busy in the kitchen. I was trying to be quiet, and I thought you were resting comfortably. I only came over to check on you. I am glad I did. You were fighting for your life. I wish I could make all these terrors go away. I pray they are only temporary."

He looked at me. "Sweetie, do you understand?"

I looked up at him. Then I asked, "Am. I. Alive?"

Matt looked puzzled but quickly realized it was a serious question. He took his time before answering. His eyes lit up, and I could tell that a million thoughts were streaming through his brain. He was trying to think of something clever to say, to make me laugh, but at last, he just pinched me! He pinched me! And then asked, "Did you feel that?" We both burst out laughing.

"Ouch!" I laughed between the shocked expression of what just happened.

"Is (pause) Aubrey home?" I asked.

"Honey, Aubrey works nights and will help you during the day while we

work out this schedule, remember?"
Matt said patiently.

I was trying to understand how grief
and love were so tightly intertwined.
Emily was on her way back to Florida,
Aubrey was quitting school and
getting a night job so she could be
with me during the day, and Matt was
trying desperately to do everything to
ensure my safety, my care. All I was
supposed to do was work hard and
focus on me. This didn't seem fair.

I glanced upward; my mouth pursed. I
was in deep thought. My eyes fixed on
something in the distance, as if in a
trance. I was looking past Matt. He
called my name. I blinked, refocused.
"Are we okay, Matty? Are you okay?"
He smiled and nodded at me. No
words, just a gentle recognition of us. I
felt lost like I was wandering out in
the pouring rain, no protection, just
standing out in the deluge of water
that escapes the sky.

Matt asked, "Mary, would you like to shower now or after dinner? I can help you."

"After. Please," I said hungrily.

Matt clapped his hands together, "Great, let's eat, I'm starving!"

He assisted me out of the chair and bypassed the walker.

"Matt." I panicked. "I can't, need walker!" I cried out, confused, no— frightened.

"Trust me. We will go slow." He wrapped his arms around my waist and said, "Okay, let's walk. Lift your right foot, no, your other right, and now your left foot. Right again. Fifteen steps and we will be to the table. You're doing great love."

I had all the grace of a three-legged dog. I wondered if perhaps my lack of coordination was a sign of something, something frightful to my mind, I couldn't help but wonder if this was permanent. I staggered to the kitchen table like a drunk. Matt was careful to guide me. Several minutes later I was tucked in at the table. Sweat dripped from my cold trembling hands. Matt reached for me. I looked down and tried to hide my hands, to wipe them on my pants.

"Mary don't be ashamed. The doctor said this might happen when you feel scared. I am sorry I scared you, but I won't let you stop trying. I don't care about your sweaty palms. I care about you!" Matt grabbed a chair and sat down next to me. "I'm sorry I made you afraid, my love. Are you afraid of the future?"

No answer.

"Is it trying to remember the past?"

I sat and stared down, trying to understand the question.

"Mookie, is it this moment? Did I scare you that much? Please say something!"

"I don't know," I whispered. "Mookie." I tried to repeat the word.

"Yes, love, I would call you my Mookie P.," Matt said patiently.

Chapter 34
Fear

What is fear? Is it a place or an imagination or a lost memory that must be imagined? Fear is a kind of madness, but one that is useful if you know how it works. Fear will take you by the hand to the things you keep and guard your precious dreams. Fear will push you. Fear will allow you to take chances, make mistakes, and along the way, get messy.

"Let's face this fear together, Mary. We will look at this with the courage and understanding it will take to win, and then we will let it go. These fears that wake you up, let them show you the way to your true self, to the brave soul whose love shines like a full moon leading the way in the darkness." Matt was so serious now. "What we have learned through all these challenges is with the fear that hides behind your eyes, our love is brighter, stronger, deeper. When you find yourself, my love, you will be your own captain, fully in charge of your future, our future. This fear you have of falling asleep will subside someday. Until then somehow you must keep fighting those demons who tried to take you. Do you understand?" Matt spoke slowly, so I could understand, "You have amazing strength. I know we will be okay because you will use this fear to make you stronger. I need you to fight, to continue to try. I watch you and even though you are scared you do it, anyway. You do it!" Matt said so patiently, so lovingly, so carefully.

I looked at him; a blue hue was flashing around him now. "Matt," I whispered. I wish I could express my thoughts more clearly; I wish I could speak the words out loud. *These feelings I have for you can't end until my body ceases to function and they release my soul for whatever comes after. If I had died that day and never returned, I would have died loved and happy. Never knowing the sadness that encased my family and still does, leaving them with a hole that would gradually be filled with a lapse of memories. I hope that somehow, they are embedded into my soul and I in theirs, that our love will endure forever. Even on my darkest days, it's my love for you that continuously drives me, keeping my mind from sinking into the dark that continues to claim me. I know that however deep in fear I've fallen, you will be there like solid ground steadying me, giving me time to climb back into positivity. Rescuing me from drowning in these horrific nightmares. You are what I live for. It's you. You are my reason for breathing. The thought of you wearing a coat of pain with the loss of me, of us, is too much to stomach, too much to bear. Someday I will tell you all of this, someday. Until then all I can say is, "Thank. You!"*

Matt served a delicious, creative meal. Sweet potatoes, steamed carrots, and grilled salmon. He said he liked the challenges. And for dessert Cheese Puffs. I smiled with a sigh and nodded my head in appreciation.

"Mary, you have outpatient therapy tomorrow morning. Aubrey and I will take you together." Matt said.

"Aaafff." Sigh… "Aaaffftt"

"After?" Matt asked.

I nodded my head. My brain was shutting down.

"After dinner would you like to shower?" he translated.

I nodded. "Shh ow er then (pause) b eee dd."

I tried to enunciate my words, to communicate in a strong voice, but my brain was foggy, my words were empty.

"After dinner, you would like to shower and then go to bed? Sweetie, it's only 7:30, are you sure?" Matt wondered.

Come on brain, use your words, I thought to myself. I took a deep breath and said, "Yes. Big. Tomorrow." Slowly, in my monotone voice. I looked over at Matt and he was grinning.

"Do you mind if I join you later? I can take a few hours and get some work done." Matt said carefully, reading my face for any signs of reluctance.

I looked straight in his eyes. "Yes!" I said in a strong voice.

"Okay, let's go then." He helped me up. This time I got to use the walker.

After the shower, he tucked me into bed, kissed me on my forehead, and with a sense of pride said, "I'll be right outside the door listening carefully in case you need me."

Sometime later, I heard him calling my name, a distant panicky, "Mary, Mary, I'm right here. I'm here!"

I woke, startled, from an ominous nightmare.

Chapter 35

Matt

A memory from Matt... Her cheeks are wet, and her body is bathed in a cold sweat. The sheets are twisted around her limbs, probably because she was thrashing in her sleep. Her heart pounds against my chest. I hold her as she trembles. I hate this for her. I hate that I can't help with her struggles. There must be something I am missing. There must be something we have not thought of. Something must help.

Mary

I heard Matt calling out my name. The room was entirely dark. No light anywhere. The remnants of my nightmare still clung to my mind, haunting me. I had trouble distinguishing between my nightmares and reality. I lay silently cradled in Matt's arms trying desperately to make out images in the room's darkness. I swallowed, trying to catch my breath from the trembling, frightened cries. Matt reached across me and turned on the lamp next to the bed.

"Is that better?" he asked, careful not to overstimulate me.

"I'm. Sorry," I tried very hard to get him to understand what I was saying. He didn't ask me to repeat myself or help me with my words.

He simply said, "Let's get some sleep."

We closed our eyes, Matt clinging to me, desperately trying to calm my left side. I lay in silent prayer.

I wake up at 6 a.m. to an empty bed. I heard Matt and Aubrey talking but couldn't make out the words. The smell of coffee and breakfast was all I needed at that moment. Another day. I worried about Matt. I had to try harder today. He needed sleep. I needed sleep. The only way he would rest was if I could do better than I had yesterday. I would try.

I sat up on my own. It took a while, but after many failed attempts, I did it. Now what? I was sitting on the edge of the bed. My walker was ten feet away.

"Good morning!" Matt entered our bedroom and smiled brightly. "It appears you are trying to conquer the day!"

"Yes!" I said clearly. My response took Matt back to a time before the pulmonary embolism, but only for a moment.

"Well, I will not stop you. Do you want to walk over to get your walker? With my help."

"Yes!" I tried to stand up but didn't have the strength yet. Matt let me try by myself and then came over and used his arms as a brace. I hung on and lifted myself out of bed! "I. Did. It!" I said in a great celebration.

"You did it!" Matt exclaimed.

Chapter 36

More Rehab

Emily had been back to school for a few weeks. We were figuring out a routine. Matt liked to go with Aubrey and me to my rehabilitation appointments but drove separately so he could head to the office.

After breakfast and a drive across town, the three of us entered rehab. Katie came out to greet us. "Good morning!" she said with a comforting smile. "Follow me."

Matt hung on to my gait belt. Aubrey reminded me to lift my feet as I clung to the walker, white-knuckled. It wasn't easy trying to manipulate my mind and body to work in unison, but it was doable. I focused on my next step as Katie said, "Mary! I am so proud of you!"

Proud of me? Why? I wondered.

We entered the windowless office and sat around the table.

Katie didn't waste any time. She pulled out the preschooler cards and said, "Shall we begin?"

I looked down at my hands, which were curled in my lap, fingers intertwined as the sweat dripped freely from them.

Katie looked at Aubrey and Matt and asked, "Has Mary done any homework?"

"Yes!" Aubrey answered quickly. "Mom, what's wrong?" she said cautiously, slowly, making sure not to overstimulate my thinking process.

I looked up and smiled and shook my head.

"Okay Mary let's start at the beginning. Will you tell me your full name?"

"Mary. Kaye. Podschweit." I whispered.

"What year is it?"

I shrugged; I didn't know.

"Not a problem. If I told you it was 2014, would that help?"

I looked over at Matt, surprised. "2014?" I said in disbelief.

"Yes, 2014. Mary, can you tell me your phone number?"

I took a moment and shook my head no.

Katie held up colored cards. "Let's work on colors."

Colors, like blue light dancing around you, the pink around Matt, and the orange around Aubrey. Those colors, I thought to myself.

The first card: *Come on brain, you know these. Tell them please, tell them.*

"Rrrrrrrrr Eeeeeeeee Dddddddd Aaa" I said. My brain had not woken up yet.

"Red. Don't put an 'a' at the end of the word and then you've got it. Let's try again: what is this color?" Katie coached me to use my words.

"Rrrreeeddddaaa"

My brain was grinding, refusing to start, refusing to get into first gear, refusing to work. I could read the words, make them out, but I was having a difficult time with articulation.

She smiled and began to write something in her book.

We went through all the basic colors. I ended every word with an 'a' sound.

Katie gave me and my family homework, and said, "I'll see you Friday. Great job Mary. I can tell you are working and getting your speech back!"

I smiled and nodded my head.

Randie knocked on the door. "I'm ready for Mary," she said.

Randie's smile could easily warm up the coldest of days.

She asked me to sit in a chair on my own. I was terrified at this request. What if I fall? I couldn't, not yet.

"What I want you to do is turn your walker, so it's square to the chair. Take a step back until you feel the seat hit the back of your legs. There you go, you're doing it!" she exclaimed in an enthusiastic tone.

I did what she asked, reluctantly at first, and then with her excitement leading the way, more deliberately. I turned, so I was in front of the chair. My walker was square with the chair and I started to step back. Soon I felt the chair contact my legs. I sat, feeling scared because it was more of a *flop* than a *sit. Thank goodness the chair didn't move while I sat down.* I looked up to see Matt and Aubrey standing there, proud, holding back the urge to cheer. Randie was beyond proud of me. I felt like a toddler taking her first steps, listening to the applause and cheers as she walks from Mommy to Daddy.

Randie asked if I could stand up on my own.

I did as she asked. It was very difficult to get my brain and body to interact, but I forced it. I forced my body to trust. I had to shut off my brain, but I stood up with the help of the walker.

"Mary," Randie said, "let's see what else you can do." She put the walker a few feet from my reach. Matt stood on one side of me and Randie on the other. Aubrey stepped in front of the walker and stood there teasing me, calling me over like a dog.

"Over here, Mom!" she whistled, which made me giggle.

I began walking without the help of my walker, wobbling back and forth before falling into the walker. Everyone clapped like it was all part of the plan. "Again," I said.

"Did you just hear Mom? She was asking if she could try again!" Aubrey celebrated this decision and once again stepped away with the walker.

"Again."

This time they took another step back, and I wobbled over. *If I were outside trying this, I might get asked if I were drunk*. The thought brought me great laughter, laughter I couldn't stop.

Just as quick as we had begun PT, it ended. Randie said, "You are doing remarkable. Same homework as before. Let's get you over to see Amber."

I had to use my walker to take the simple steps over to OT, but in my mind, I was planning for the day when I would no longer use help to walk.

Amber was all business again. Right off the bat, she asked me if I was showering on my own.

"No," I answered.

"Brushing your hair?" she asked.

"No," I said.

"How about your personal hygiene? Are you able to do anything unassisted?" She stood up and put her hands on the table in front of me.

215

"No," I said, rather ashamed now.

"Matt and Aubrey, Mary has to relearn, and you are not helping anyone, especially her, if you continue to persist in helping her. She has to learn how to manage this on her own!" Amber scolded.

I shut everything out as she continued to chastise my family.

I sat there, and I wondered what I would have to do to become more independent.

I looked across the room and saw the brightest-looking baby dressed in primrose pajamas. She had a pair of soft shoes on, the ones parents use for baby's first shoes, the ultra-thin ones you can still feel the ground through. We made eye contact, and she squealed in delight. Her little smile could light up the whole town. Her little smile was contagious. The little girl giggled, waving her arms for the pick-up she knew was coming, but before she was hoisted high, she wobbled and fell on her bottom. She was giggling in delight.

I think it's scenes like that that kept me knowing I was alive. I needed these little reminders that people were inherently good and loving; otherwise, the tide of depression and self-doubt would sweep me away into some fearful and narrow-minded thought pattern. I never wanted to be like that, and I still don't; I never wanted to doubt my existence. Not like I did in my nightmares, where I felt as though nothing was real and yet, everything was real.

Confusion must have masked my face, because Amber politely said, "Mary, understand, I am not being mean. I believe in you and I know you can do everything I ask of you."

I smiled and nodded my head.

"I'll see you on Friday," Amber said in a matter-of-fact tone.

We made our way to the car. Aubrey was excited about the progress she had seen today and continued to discuss the game plan with Matt. I sat there, zoned out of the conversation, zoned out from life, trying to decide what to do next. How could I practice getting better, to live so my family could live too? This was very important to me.

Chapter 37
A Social Gathering

"The office is having a small party Saturday night. I have been asked if we could come over for a bit. I told them I might convince you to go out, especially to say thank you. Everyone from the office would love to see you!" Matt said hopefully.

To see me. Me? I wondered why anyone would want to see me, to remember the person I used to be. Matt needed to be social. He has always been an extrovert. I smiled and nodded my head yes.

We got home; the house felt cold, empty. Matt sensed it too. I knew he couldn't just sit here watching the walls and monitoring my every movement. He needed to see real people, to talk and laugh, to be engaging, to listen to others share their stories and jokes. They gave him energy I couldn't give him right now. I thought I used to love being around

people, like Matt, but now? Nope. I
didn't know if it was because I was
embarrassed about what I have
transformed into or scared that
someone would bump into me. Fear is
ugly.

I decided I must do this for Matt. I
must show him I was on his team. The
last week of February was cold and
gray. Even on sunny days everything
seemed dull. An outing might be nice,
might be safe.

"We won't go for very long, honey. Just
enough time to say hi, maybe have a
drink, and then we will leave. Thanks
for doing this. With Aubrey having to
work nights, I could not leave you
alone. I want you to understand how
proud I am," Matt said.

I was happy. Life is precious. I was
glad we got to share this journey
together. I wanted to make Matt
proud. I needed him to be happy.
Before my brain injury, I split my time
between work responsibilities and
family. I put myself at the bottom of

my priorities. And now, I had to slow down and relearn how to... well, everything. The great news was, though, that my therapist believed I can, and I will continually get better. Matt, Aubrey, and Emily, my loves, my tribe, they fed my soul. At one time, I never met a stranger, everyone became friends. Now, I needed and looked for the quiet joys of life, a bit of peace. But I had to let go of my fears and be a supportive wife. I had to do things I didn't want to do, because my family has made so many incredible sacrifices for me.

"I look forward to seeing everyone," I whispered with a smile.

Matt came over to where I was seated, wrapped my face in his hands and kissed me. "Thank you for trying, for me."

Chapter 38
Date Night Disaster

Matt helped me get ready. He carefully applied mascara, foundation, blush, and lipstick. He dressed me in real clothes. I couldn't think of the last time I hadn't worn sweatpants and a baggy sweatshirt. He brushed my hair and pinned up the sides. I looked sullen, but he said I looked beautiful. He sprayed me with a fresh-scented cologne and asked if I remembered the last time, I got dressed up to go out.

I shook my head no.

He looked in the closet for shoes and decided on UGG boots. They would keep my feet warm and the traction was good. He got my pink coat with the shiny black buttons and a fun scarf, matching hat, and gloves and declared I was ready to take on the night!

He buckled me in, put my walker in the trunk, and off we went. As excited as he was, I was just as scared.

We parked in the handicapped spot close to the door. He undid my seatbelt, kissed me quickly on the cheek, and said joyfully, "Ready?"

I smiled back and nodded my head.

We stepped in and were swarmed by people. They were hugging, kissing, and celebrating seeing us out together. Someone had saved us seats by the door, with drinks on the table. The excitement was overwhelming. My brain wasn't as brave as I wanted it to be. Words and smells assaulted my senses. I wondered if they remembered the real me, who I used to be. Maybe that's all they knew, the old me. Everyone was very nice and friendly. They shared stories but all I could do was nod in agreement.

My ears began to close, my throat tightened, and my breathing became shallow, but no one noticed. A heavy cloud enveloped my space and I could no longer see. I was caught up in a crowd of friends I didn't recognize. I didn't know what was happening. My hands began to sweat, a cold obnoxious sweat. I shut down. Someone recognized this as a symptom of brain injury and told someone to get Matt. People started stepping away. All I could do was sit and try to hold back the tears.

My doctor had said I had signs of social anxiety, but I had never bothered to listen. It's a pain I could not explain or conquer. With all the other obstacles I had to face social anxiety seemed like a monster.

A few people helped us out and got me buckled into the safety, the quiet of the car. Matt was just outside my door. Friends were coming out and apologizing, giving hugs and handshakes. Feeling defeated, I cried unapologetically. I mourned what we once had. I mourned for my husband and the relationship we once had that was now gone.

We began to drive. Matt pulled over, looked at me lovingly, apologetically, and then drove home without speaking a word. He parked the car in the garage, grabbed the walker from the trunk, and helped me out of the car and into the house. Silence.

I didn't know what he was thinking. My fear was that he was second-guessing us. Everything bad was going through my mind. I wished for the past, wondering if it would have been better if I had just died and not come back. I was swimming in self-pity, self-doubt. I tried to make eye contact with Matt, but he removed my coat and helped me sit down on the love seat, then removed my boots in silence.

It was terribly frustrating not being able to communicate. It seemed like my unruly left side was laughing at me. How utterly ridiculous I was for trying to be a wife to Matt. His companion. His soul mate. I sat there feeling ashamed.

Matt came back in his pj's, carrying a makeup wipe. He carefully removed the mask he had applied earlier that evening. First, he cleansed the right side of my face and then he gently kissed my right cheek. Then the left side and again, gently kissed my left cheek. Worked his way to my left eye and kissed my eyelid. Worked his way to the right eye and gently kissed my right eyelid. Still no words.

We sat in silence, holding each other in heartache, mourning what was.

Chapter 39

Medical Marijuana

"Sweetie, I have been talking to Ken about your involuntary muscle movement. His mother-in-law recently passed away. She was very sick and the only rest she had was from taking a tincture." Matt said carefully.

"Ken said it helped with her trembling. How would you feel if we tried it? I want to give you some rest from your left side. He drove down earlier today and dropped it off. He said to give it to you before bed. It will help you sleep."

It scared me. Medicine got me here. Now Matt was suggesting I should take something that could make it worse?

Matt said, "I'll take it with you, if you want me to, just to try it together." Finally, he was talking to me. How pitiful of an existence where I live in my damaged mind.

I knew he was trying to help and that he would never want to harm me. I smiled and nodded my head yes.

Matt looked surprised. "Okay, we will do this together. Ken recommended we put it in hot tea before bed. I'll make us some tonight."

My days and hours had become wrapped into one. A routine was important. I understood that, at least I tried. I found myself crying and confused more often. It scared me to be out of control. My left side was a constant reminder that I was damaged.

Matt made me hot tea and put a drop of tincture in the amber steaming cup. He moved across the room gracefully, carefully carrying the hot cup like a professional waiter. He placed it on the side table with instructions to not burn me. The cup was half full. I looked at Matt, confused. He smiled, bent down, and kissed me on my forehead.

Matt shrugged and said, "I want you to be successful. With half of cup I am betting you can do this on your own. I'll help you lift it up, but I am confident you can do this."

My left side didn't agree with him. It was difficult to maintain my balance. It was worse at night, if you can imagine. My left side would move violently, causing my entire body to go off-kilter. Everything was more difficult at night. I looked forward to being able to enjoy the quiet nights, the ones of still telephones and the rhythmic Tick-Tock of clocks. I loved the random sounds that came from my family; the nightly chatter from birds, the sway of the evergreen trees. I really enjoyed those nights with the subtle background noises. Matt hung on tightly to my left arm and we sat in silence enjoying the peace and tranquility of the evening. If it weren't for my left side taking up so much life, I could do more, to try.

"We. Need. Name her!" I said.

"Name who, Mary?" Matt said with a puzzled look.

"Left side." My voice was raspy, like an old woman, even though I was young. "Is my diaphragm damaged? Why can't I speak?"

"Maybe this tea will help. You are relearning how to use your diaphragm again. I am glad you aren't giving up and I won't either. It's no one's fault tonight. We will have other opportunities," Matt said.

We drank tea. Matt opted out of trying the tincture just in case I needed him, but he made tea to drink with me, never wanting me to be alone.

"Sleepy?" he asked.

I nodded my head yes. The only thing that could save me from the demons of my yesterday, of my tomorrow, was sleep, and I hadn't had a good night's rest since November 20, 2013. I prayed the tincture will work. I prayed for rest. I prayed for a dreamless sleep.

My doctor said that I needed to rest. She didn't want to give me any drugs for fear of them doing the opposite. Now, I was so desperate I had chosen a very controversial method. Tincture is a liquid form of marijuana.[1]

Matt thought the taste would be too bitter for me, so he added a dab of honey to the sleepy time tea. We hoped that it would help relax my left side enough for a good rest.

I wanted to rest. Perhaps with a rested mind, I would have the sharpness to make the decisions that could be the difference in my rehabilitation. Now I could not make it past three thirty a.m. without waking up scared, frightened, lost. Usually I remained in fear, willing myself to return to sleep, as unpleasant as it was. Randie, my PT, has explained that exercise, healthy food, and proper hygiene would help with my personal organization of each day. For this to happen, I had to control my left side.

My left side had a mind of its own. Independent, stubborn, and strong. Ginger from *Gilligan's Island* was a stunning, independent redhead. Yes, Ginger. *I shall call her Ginger. A part of me that exists because of this injury.*

"Ginger." I said as I closed my eyes. "Ginger, I like it!"

Those painful memories I had when I closed my eyes, memories of a broken time spent in the hospital, are just the same as nightmares. They vanished when I awoke. I struggled to understand when I was here in the present moment or when I was dreaming of a false reality. Once I opened my eyes, let in daylight, they had no choice but to leave, and I could let in all the wonderful things around me. I would begin with gratitude. I hoped this would help keep me immersed in love, in reality.

"Goodnight Ginger!"

Chapter 40
Ginger

"There you are! I was wondering if you'd wake up! I messed up, I'm sorry. I kept on waking up to make sure you were breathing. You didn't have any bad dreams last night? Sweetie, can you talk to me?" Matt asked apologetically.

"Yes. Slept! Matt, I slept! I slept!" I tried to sit up on my own and did so with some effort and trial. Matt continued to stare. My left side was moving but much less than the day before.

"Mary Kaye, do you notice anything?"

I looked puzzled.

"Your left side is remarkably calm, there's still involuntary muscle movement, but so much better."

"Ginger," I whispered.

"Ginger! Like from *Gilligan's Island*? That's brilliant, Mary. Let's get you up to start your day."

Matt helped me to the kitchen table and served breakfast.

I shared with him I wanted green foods. But the look of disappointment on his face broke my heart. "Maybe for lunch and dinner?" I said with a smile.

Matt matter-of-factly said, "Aubrey is sleeping in; she closed last night, and we all know how important sleep is. I'd like to let her sleep for as long as possible. I need to run to the office when she gets up. I won't be gone long." Matt looked at me and saw how scared I've become. "Mary, everything will work out. I know it's scary, but I will never leave you. I understand you are frightened I won't return. Is this right?"

I nodded my head yes.

"How about I call you when I get to the office and I will call again when I leave the office. But we must work together. Would you agree?"

I nodded my head.

"I will also have to go to the grocery store to get you green foods!" Matt replies with a twinkle in his eyes. "Green, hmmm, *Green Eggs and Ham*? Maybe you could practice reading while I am gone?

You know our friend Scott Schaefer has a similar disorder? Except with his food can't touch each other. Everything has to be separated."

I stared at him, trying to comprehend what was just said. I finally had to ask, "Matt, does Scott have a brain injury?"

Oh, my goodness. If we could only laugh so freely every day as we did at that moment.

It was a laughter that Matt could feel in his lungs, so hard that it took his breath away. The lack of oxygen didn't matter. All the anguish of the past few days melted like snowballs in a sudden heatwave. This laughter created a small vacation, a blessed relief from all the distress that shoved its way into our lives. For a single moment, the lack of money to pay the stack of medical bills did not matter. The how-to list shoved in the corner and his to-do list, which kept getting longer, didn't matter at that moment. He lost the tightness in his chest. The muscles in his neck relaxed. After all that had occurred, he felt hope. And hope felt good. With hope came the thought "things would turn around," that somehow, he could use this as an inspiration. That the person he thought was dead and brought back to life had a story to tell. He felt joy ride into his life alongside the laughter. And Matt knew that when the laughter left, this joy would stay with him, with us.

I lifted my head and stared in delight at my beautiful husband. I sighed in satisfaction. I had just found a piece of this puzzle I had spent 75 days solving. A smile spread across my face.

Aubrey zipped up the stairs with a look of trepidation.

"What's going on? Is everything okay?" She blurted out.

She saw us both gasping for breath and quickly realized that we were laughing and not crying like she had first thought.

"I thought you were crying! It scared me to death! Sorry, Mom, I didn't mean to...."

Matt and I both burst out laughing!

I repeated, "Death a!"

The three of us laughed so hard now, it was hard to breathe. I began coughing and couldn't stop. My face became red. Matt realized my laughter was triggering a panic attack. He stopped immediately, bent down, put his hands on my knees, and coached me to breathe. Aubrey ran and grabbed a cold washcloth.

"That escalated quickly," Matt said. "You're okay, sweetie. I see Ginger is awake again."

"Who's Ginger?" Aubrey asked, puzzled.

I looked up and forced a smile.

"Your mom thought she should name her left side. And somehow came up with Ginger. I think it fitting, don't you, Aubrey?" Matt expressed with great delight at the cleverness of the name.

Aubrey and Matt went over a game plan for the day. Matt would run to the office and then to the grocery store for everything green. "I hope you like lime Jell-O." Matt said as he was making a grocery list.

Aubrey and I smiled at each other.

"Mom, I was talking to a coworker last night, and he had a good idea. Do you remember my friend Em? Em purchased you a wipe and write board that will help you relearn how to write numbers and letters. I hope you will try. It was very thoughtful." Aubrey said with gratitude.

I smiled and nodded my head.

"I'll call when I get to the office and then before I leave for the store. Let me know if we need anything else." Matt came over and kissed us both on the forehead before he left.

"Let me clear off the table and clean the kitchen, then we will begin our day of in-home rehab." Aubrey said with a loving spirit of hope.

Chapter 41

Doctor Aubrey

With quick work, Aubrey helped me get settled in for in-home rehab. She pulled out flashcards with colors and animals with simple names like cat, dog, bird, and numbers. I knew the answers, but I had a difficult time articulating them. She had a timer set so I would be challenged but not overstimulated.

Next up, PT. Honestly, she was a natural.

She turned on YouTube and we began the walking video. While hanging onto the walker, I practiced walking in place and bending down in a squat. I lifted my arms over my head while Aubrey hung on to my gait belt. Difficult work.

And for the final challenge, OT.

We made our way to the bathroom. Aubrey helped me apply toothpaste on my toothbrush and prepared one for herself. Her smile was soft, gentle like beautiful flower petals captured in a warm breeze. "Ready, Mom?"

She picked up her toothbrush and instructed me to follow along. In a circular motion, we began with the lower back and made our way around until we were finished, ending in the top. She handed me a disposable cup halfway filled with water. "Okay, now we will rinse. Try not to swallow; we will spit it out into the sink."

I followed along, trying to mimic Aubrey. When she spit into the sink, I spit down the front of my sweatshirt. Ashamed, I said, "I'm a. Sorry!"

Aubrey just shrugged and said, "Let's change your shirt. Don't worry; you tried, and that's all we can ask for. You are doing great."

After the change of clothes, she escorted me back into the dining room and sat me down at the table. Continuing with OT, she pulled out the write and wipe boards with different colors of dry erase markers. "Which color do you want to use first, Mom?"

I point at the green one.

"Use your words; pointing doesn't count!" Her smile alone was something to cherish.

I smiled back and said "Gr (pause) een a."

"Mom, 'green,' can you say 'green'? You are putting an 'a' at the end of the word. Let's try again."

"Gggrrreeennn a." I tried to repeat it without the 'a,' but to no avail.

"Mom, I'm proud of you for trying. Pick up the green marker and let's start with letters and work our way to numbers if we have the time."

I did as I was instructed. I tried to remove the cap but my left side, Ginger, was not cooperating.

I handed the marker over to Aubrey.

"What do you want me to do?" she asked patiently.

247

"Please remove the cap," I pleaded.

Thirty minutes went by quickly. I was exhausted.

Aubrey affectionately said, "Mom, let's sit you in the by the sunny window. I bet you would like that."

I nodded my head.

"Nope, I don't understand gestures, you must use your words." Aubrey encouraged.

"Yes, thank you." I stammered.

"Without the walker. It's only a few steps and I will hold your gait belt."

I wanted her to be successful. So many sacrifices. So much care. I did as she asked, and we made our way to the chair by the window.

"Would you like the television, music, or quiet today?" Aubrey asked after helping me to my seat.

I smiled up at her and with a bit of mischief I pointed at the television and said "TV!"

She put in a movie with the volume on low, then tucked me in with a soft blanket. She brought me a water bottle, set it on the side table, and kissed me gently on my forehead.

"Mom, I need to shower. I'll use yours since it's close by. Will you be okay for 15 minutes? I don't want you to be running off!" Now her smile was playful.

I began to nod my head yes, then saw disappointment. I corrected myself and said, "Yes, I'll be fine."

She was beaming with accomplishment.

A movie. How normal. I looked outside. The reflection caught my gaze in the window beside me; as I stared, so did my reflection. She was pale, with mousy brown hair and sad eyes. Everything about her was dark. Her expression, her furrowed brows, her lips... had I always been this way? I used to be kind, didn't I? Wasn't I supposed to look bright, not so worn out? My eyes were supposed to express happiness, not fear. If people saw me this way, how would they know who I really was? How was anybody supposed to get to know the real me—or who I used to think I was? I missed my old self. I was afraid she was gone forever.

I heard Aubrey speaking with Matt. He was on his way home. Soon she joined me with a pillow and a throw and fell asleep on the couch.

The sound of her sleeping was rewarding. I zoned out from watching the TV and stared at her, remembering her as an infant. I tried to recall when her bright blue eyes first found mine and her first laugh, as only a baby can laugh, a sweet sound, unblemished by the hurts of life. Her perfect little face glowed from a light within, and her miniature fingers grasped mine and held tight. She knew! Somehow it felt like she knew I would need her as an adult. Somehow during all this confusion, she provided me with comfort. I remembered! I remembered now! When Matt first held our wailing newborn baby, he began singing our song, and she cooed! A very happy, very content baby. My Aubrey. The one whose life was derailed by my injury lay sleeping on the couch. I get to love her. How blessed we are to have the ability to love unconditionally. Somehow, I believed she knew I needed joy in the midst of my pain. At a hectic and frightening time in our lives, she met my whirlwind of fear with a sense of safety. She believed in me!

Matt walked through the door with groceries. I was sure everything he had bought was green. I hoped this was not a permanent quirk. The doctors couldn't answer that. Only time would tell. Until then, Matt had taken on the challenge of trying to satisfy my fascination with monochromatic foods.

"Hi, sweetie!" He put the groceries on the kitchen counter and made his way across the room to give me a kiss. He saw Aubrey sleeping. A beautiful smile spread across his face; he raised a finger to his lips as if to silence me.

We both smiled. He went back into the kitchen and put away the groceries as quietly as possible, then returned to sit in the black leather recliner. "Nap time?" he asked.

"Yes, nap time!" And I closed my eyes.

Chapter 42

Green

My brain was on five percent battery; exhaustion had set in. It appeared Matt and Aubrey felt the same way. I sat in the sunlight, letting it warm my face. The fireplace was on and as comfortable as I was; I was fighting sleep. I opened my eyes to make sure I was not alone. Aubrey and Matt were taking some well-deserved time to rest and soak in the calm peace of this lazy afternoon. I carried an enormous burden of guilt. My family assistance was freely given. Yet at what cost? I couldn't comprehend how I would overcome the obstacles in front of me. What would it cost my family to keep sacrificing for me? I was tired… so very, exhausted. *Come on brain, finish the thought process. Use your words... say it out loud. Another time, then. Now sit quietly and enjoy the peace of the moment.*

We were settling into a routine, a much-needed routine.

I could function better because of the tincture, but once it wore off Ginger was in full swing. She startled me from my half-sleep. I tightly hugged my left arm, willing it to calm down.

The sun was dipping behind the horizon, but the daylight still lingered in the air as though accidentally left behind. It was a cold and cloudless night. I took my eyes off the luminous sky and was startled to see Matt staring at me. Our eyes embraced, and we both smiled, content to just be. To sit in the silence.

Aubrey must have left for work. She had maneuvered quietly around the house in order not to wake us. So very considerate.

Matt joined me in the oversized chair by the window. We sat in silence, looking outside, watching the long shadows of the evening dissolve into the gathering darkness of the nighttime. Peaceful. As he was holding me, he reached and caressed my face, cupped it to fit the frame of his gentle hands. He kissed me tenderly on the lips and whispered in my ear, "I love you like a fat kid likes cake!"

We burst out laughing! "Oh, Matty!" I said in my monotone hoarse whisper.

I glanced at Matt. The corners of his lips were fighting a smile, his eyebrows slightly raised. I looked away before that mischievous look of his spread. His exuberance was contagious. But before I could strengthen my resolve, I'd already glanced upward. In a few seconds, that pirate-like grin of his was on my face too. We both erupted in a fit of giggling.

After moments of laughter, Matt asked, "Hungry?"

I replied, "Yes."

"Still want green foods?" he asked with a sweet grin.

"Yes," I said.

Green. I liked the color, the shades, the smell. I smelled green. Hmmm...

freshly cut grass, pine needles, a crisp green apple. I smelled these. Well, this was interesting. None of these things were in front of me now, but I remembered. I remembered!

Green can be the best color. Everything depends on context. I imagined a forest, fresh spring plants after winter, or my mother's summer garden with her purple iris blossoming on long green blades. Green was beautiful. I wanted everything to be a verdant shade. I wanted to paint my house spring green, accent with pots glazed in forest pine, and wear a scarf of hunter green. How about sea-foam green for the bath? I sat and wondered about how this color made me feel. It was exciting to taste and smell this color I was thinking of. Oh... a fresh green salad! Yes, I wanted a crispy green salad.

Matt yelled from the kitchen where he was making us dinner. "I hope a salad is okay. You know, it's rather difficult to make a green meal!" he said teasingly.

It was a kitchen sink salad, or rather, everything was in it but the kitchen sink. There was lettuce, cucumber, green tomato, green apple, pistachios, toasted seeds, fresh herb leaves, blue cheese, celery, and green peppers. The salad was tossed in a rich creamy cucumber dressing and served with fresh green beans. Delicious. Fresh. Just what I longed for.

After dinner we showered, and he served me my hot tea with the tincture. It worked quickly. Soon I was tucked into bed.

Chapter 43

Choices Cannot Be Undone

Have you ever had a dream so real it confused you when you woke up? This time I was calm. I was alone with my dad. We were sitting in one of those uncomfortable hospital chairs in ICU. It was an oversized sky blue/gray vinyl chair. There was no beeping from the monitors. Everything was unplugged. A few nurses came to write a report, and they sent the cleaning crew to clean the room as someone else was there to prepare my body for its next adventure. Dad and I were sitting quietly, staring at the shell that was once me. Dad grabbed my hand and asked if I remembered that I was not supposed to be here. "You're supposed to be with Matt and your girls. You never finished your job."

"I am supposed to be with Matt and our girls?" I looked at him and saw the pain on his face. "Dad," I said, "What happened? Why am I here?"

He looked down at our hands, grasped mine a little tighter and said, "Sweetie, my Mary, God was sending you back, but you refused, and now I am here. I'll do my best to help you out of the darkness, but you have to decide."

I repeated to my dad, wisdom from Matt, "Choices cannot be undone. Words and actions cannot be taken back." I understood now, I said, head drooping, sleepy.

Death came to me with slow rattling gasps, through the breathing tube, my mouth opened wide. The same rattling gasps that had taken my father years before. My breathing would stop for a time only to restart, like a drowning victim coming up for one last breath. But in a few moments, I will have passed on, my earthly body dead. Detached, I watched the hectic activity in the room dive into calmness.

"Once when I was a little girl, I dreamt that the grass in our backyard was an orangish yellow. The orange grass rose into the sky, leaving perfect green grass orange underneath. It painted the sky perfect shades of oranges, yellows, and blues. I was dancing outside, twirling round and round. The grass was soft and squishy. That morning I didn't wake up sleepily, but instantly, like a switch had been flipped. I ran from my bed to the backyard. And you know what? The grass was green, and the sky was blue. I asked everyone where the orange grass had gone, but since I was little everyone just played along. I cried that I wasn't making it up, and everyone just stared with knowing smiles and nods. No one could tell me it wasn't real; I'd 'seen it' happen. I would lie in the soft grass staring up at the sky. Outside was the proof. Now when I see the amazing orange in the sky, I always think of that moment. Seeing is believing, right? I guess that's why I'm so comfortable talking to you. I can see you here with me. You aren't solid yet, but Dad, I remember that moment."

Dad listened carefully. He then asked if I was ready.

"Ready? Ready for what?" I replied, puzzled.

"To go back," he breathed. "To go back home now. You have a family that is waiting for you."

Is there such a thing as a beautiful body when death has claimed the soul? There is no romantic corpse. Death is death. The flesh rots, the bones follow, the hair mats. It is life that is beautiful, a life we cherish, the soul we nurture.

"You are supposed to live. Be the wife to Matt and mother to your girls. You have a story to share, find your voice."

"Dad, it's too late. I made the wrong decision. I should have listened. What do I do now?" I said mournfully.

Dad was becoming invisible. There was just a hint of an outline now. He kissed me on my forehead and said, "Live. Live and tell your story. Live." His ghostly outline was drifting away.

263

"Live." And just like that, he was gone, in his place the beeping of the machines and Matt's voice. Yes, I could hear Matt speaking. "I'm here! I'm here!"

My life was like a black and white horror picture and I was forever being chased by the monster, the monster of death. No matter where I hid the monster was always there, clawing, gnashing, slowly finding his way to my hiding places.

I couldn't speak. *Come on Mary, let him know you stayed. You stayed to be with him.* I began moving my hand. Why couldn't I speak? Something was down my throat. I wanted to cough; I wanted to scream, but I couldn't. I reached out to his voice, but I couldn't move. *Oh, dear God, what has happened? Move your hands, come on move; move your hands. Wiggle a finger, that's it, wiggle your fingers. Matt, please see my hands move.* I heard someone calling my name. I opened my eyes and tried to find a voice. I couldn't move my head. I was tied down and gagged. What happened?

"Mary, Mary, sweetie, I'm here! I'm here!" Matt reached up and grabbed me, wrapped his sturdy arms around me. "I'm here! Talk to me, say something, please! Anything!"

"I'm. Okay!" I said, gasping through the tears running down my cheeks across his arms. "I'm (gasping) okay!" I repeated.

I wake up at 6:00 a.m. to an empty bed. I heard Matt and Aubrey talking in the kitchen. Rehab was at 7:30 a.m. Matt was going over today's care schedule. Aubrey never complained about being my voice, my chauffeur, my medic and always, my love. Matt was very confident in her abilities to always do the right thing at the right time.

At 6:15 Matt came into our room to wake me and get me going for the day. Our daily routine was simple.

6:15 up and get ready for the day

6:30 finish up in the bathroom

6:45 Breakfast

7:00 Brush teeth

M-W-F

7:05 leave for rehab with Aubrey

7:30–8:30 Speech, PT, and OT

T-TH

7:30 begin at-home rehab. Walking videos, stretching videos on YouTube

Throughout the day I work with Aubrey on reading, writing, memory, and physical activity.

After Matt left for work, I hesitantly asked Aubrey if she could help me with a little project. Before knowing what, I wanted, she said, "Yes Mom."

Chapter 44

Love Notes

Matt's love language is acts of service. Hmmm... what could I do? I could make him his lunches for work. *Me in the kitchen*, I chuckled to myself. I had to remember to ask Aubrey for her help. I could write him love notes. That would mean practicing holding a pen again. The thought of this was exciting and sad. I didn't know how to feel.

Alone with Aubrey, I asked her if she thought this was a good idea.

"Aubrey, I want to make Dad breakfast and lunches for his work and hide love notes in his lunchbox. Can you help me?" I asked almost reluctantly, because she was already doing so much.

She beamed at the idea. "Let's begin to write them today, and I can help with his lunchbox!"

Occupational therapy now comprised writing. Handwriting was one of the first skills we learned as elementary school students, after the ABC's and 123's. Most of us remember those thick pencils and the wide-lined writing paper we used in our beginner handwriting lessons. We remember the pride we felt when we first learned to write our names. Unfortunately, I had lost the ability to write. I used a whiteboard at home practicing, but it's difficult to follow the lines.

My handwriting, like my speech, was a slow process. The "Love Notes" I wrote are impossible to read, but Matt shared with us the complete joy he felt when he received them. To him, what mattered was not how illegible my handwriting was, but the thought and care it took to create each one.

Pictured are the very first "Love Notes" given to Matt

269

Chapter 45
Six Months of Trying

Our nightly routine of tincture and hot tea helped ease the involuntary muscle movement and nightmares. I continued to gasp for air and my left hand was usually balled up in a fist. Our neurologist, Dr. K, explained that these side effects were permanent, and that it would be best for us to make it normal. Normal? I didn't want any of this to become me. The stares from strangers, the whispers, the questions of "What's wrong with her, is she drunk?" would be normal now?

"We can't dwell on things we have no control over." Matt provided the warmest hug.

Aubrey was continuing to work at night and care for me during the day.

I reflected on her life, the young life of my oldest daughter Aubrey. My love, who was sacrificing her own ambitions to keep me safe, to ensure I was taken care of. I trusted in her ability to think and decide for me, knowing that we based those decisions on good. I needed routine, and she never complained; she just did.

We were a few months into this routine; progress was slow, but everyone was excited about the potential. Therapy was becoming stagnant: six months of therapy three days a week when all I wanted was to be left alone. I went to therapy and did my homework, but sadness was my companion and a smile was my disguise.

Chapter 46
Finding Me

At home, I began refusing to use of the walker. Matt reluctantly agreed; with the condition I would continue to wear the gait belt. I would practice walking unusually slowly, almost robotically, as if my brain was struggling to tell each foot to take the next step.

Matt always made time for my doctor's appointments. He liked Dr. G, and she respected him for his care of me and our daughters.

Dr. G, always kind, suggested a service dog. A dog would help me get out of the house and help me with doors or with picking items up from the floor. It astonished me at the stupidity of the suggestion. I couldn't take care of a dog. I couldn't even take care of myself! I shook my head no.

Matt carefully said, "Honey, a dog would be very helpful. I think it's a great idea."

I held back the emotions that were stuck in my throat. "No, I can't."

Dr. G and Matt began talking about the benefits. Matt gave my doctor the go-ahead.

Dr. G explained, "It will take a few years, especially since your injury is not military-related. Mary, I think you will be thankful once you get help. You have a difficult time with being social, which I understand. You are uncomfortable around everyone except for your family. A service dog will get you out and hopefully on your own. I can tell you are doubting your own abilities, but I see in front of me, a tenacious wife and mother. Someone who is strong, capable of doing great things. I want you to see this in you."

Matt and Dr. G talked about many things that morning. I zoned out. The longer I sat there the angrier I became. I hated that walker. I saw it as a reminder I had to rely on a device to walk again. I vaguely heard Dr. G. explain how art therapy would be a great tool to wake up the brain and express myself. She asked the nurse to get us information on the Brain Injury Alliance.

"I can't!" I blurted out.

Matt reached for my hand, trying to understand why I was angry at that moment. He had never seen this side of me, the side that I had been willing to keep silent, to keep buried. I hated all of this! I wanted my old life back; I wanted to remember.

I felt like I would explode as the frustration built. Matt knelt in front of me and instructed me to take a deep breath. I wanted to shout, to have a tantrum and fall on my hands and knees and beat the ground like a toddler. I wanted to vent, to let it out, but I didn't want to say words I didn't mean. I didn't want to be hurtful. I was so conflicted at this moment. Wouldn't it be easier to be cruel? But the damage would already progress into hurt. Hurting people I love. I was certain he felt the same way:

frustrated, angry, lost in our new life. I wanted to say, "Wouldn't it be better if I just died?" So many times, I've wanted to unsay things, to take them back. I was learning how to deal with it, but slowly, getting my breath back. I opened my eyes and looked at Matt. His eyes were blue today. There was a pink light surrounding him. Pink! "Let's breathe together," he said. He was like a magic elixir. He grabbed my sweaty hands and instructed me to breathe in through my nose and out of my mouth. He did the same thing.

All the while the doctor was there taking notes. Matt sensed I was going to act out again and squeezed my hand. "Look at me, Mary, breath with me!"

Dr. G. apologized for not being able to stay and told us to take our time. "I can't give her any medicine, but I know art therapy will be a great benefit. I will keep you updated on a service dog." And just like that, she was gone.

Chapter 47
No More Walker!?

I couldn't stop the hysterical crying. I don't think I've ever had an outburst like this one, in which my need to draw a breath only interrupted the screaming sobs. It was a primal sound, one of an infant, one you could not ignore. A nurse came into the room and Matt sent her away. Matt was caught between the impulse to help and letting me emote, knowing, sensing, that whatever he chose, it would alter his day. Being so close to such pain from someone you love changes a person, even if temporarily. His own pain came a little closer to the surface; it triggered his empathy. He too has lost the life we once shared, the freedom. Yet he stayed. To comfort. To love the unlovable, me.

I lost all sense of time. We could have been in the office for five minutes or an hour. I had no idea. I knew it exhausted me. Matt was very reassuring and comforting. We made

279

our way to the car and then home. He guided me over to the black recliner, covered me in a blanket, and kissed my forehead.

Feeling defeated and drained, I told Matt between breaths, "No more walker!"

He smiled and said, "I believe you can, and you will walk unassisted. But not today. At home, I agree, no walker. Out in public? Not yet, love."

I got mad. "I am an adult. I can make this decision on my own!" I broke down crying again, not out of sadness, but more out of frustration, of fear.

Matt was taken aback. "Mary, listen here! I am working hard at figuring this out. I need you on my side. I would never want to hold you back, but you have to trust me!"

I had to think, to put things into perspective. I sat there quietly. Matt pulled up a dining room chair and sat next to me. There are lots of folks who could talk the talk and put on a show, but Matt walked the walk. His integrity, his love for me, and trust in us was what I could hang onto. I had faith in him, in his leadership and decisions. I didn't know what had come over me. I looked at him; his eyes were green, and the pink danced around him. With my right hand, I hung on to my left side as Ginger threw her tantrum; she was not happy with me right now. "Matt," I softly whispered. He leaned in closer and kissed my left cheek. "I'm sorry."

Chapter 48

Words and Actions

Before I could say anything else, he put a finger on my lips. "I know, it's okay. A lot has changed. We have no control over what has happened, but we have a choice how we deal with it. I am doing the best I can, and I know you see this; I believe you understand. Mary, sweetie, there are two paths. The right and the left. Both look the same. But the outcome is different. We cannot undo choices. We cannot take words and actions back. We both seem broken right now. This path is broken. But we will find the right path. Let me pray for you, for us, right now. Is that okay?"

I nodded my head yes. I repeated to myself over and over again, "Choices cannot be undone. We cannot take words and actions back. We cannot undo choices. We cannot take words and actions back." I sat silently as Matt reached for my hands and began praying, "Dear Heavenly Father, allow

283

us the grace and forgiveness we need to heal our breaking hearts right now. Grant us the ability to keep the faith. To provide a foundation as we figure this life out. We cannot do this alone. You have been a beacon of light, of love and you brought Mary back to us. Lord, give her the strength and courage she needs to be stronger in love, stronger in faith, and knowing that she is not alone, nor am I. We seek your wisdom and we trust you. Thank you for giving us to each other. In your name we pray, Amen."

"Amen," I said.

Matt, you use your gifts for love, peace, and healing. You are my world and I know that I love you and you me and no matter what, I will fight for you. I will do whatever it takes to get better. I promise I will keep my faith; I will keep my emotions in check because I love you!

I wish I could tell him, but I must show him now. No more outbursts, no more doubting. I had to learn to control

these emotions; they were not
helping.

Chapter 49

Dream of Independence

I fell asleep in the black recliner. I dreamed of walking again. I kept walking, climbing mountains, and even running. I celebrated every step of independence, even though everyone said the dream was only a dream. Dreams can come true. Just dream and know what it means— strong hearts, brave souls, caring family and friends. All this was obtainable. The walker, my walker, stood beside me, taunting me, laughing at my foolish dream, but today, even though I must use it, I dream of the day when it will collect dust in the corner.

Chapter 50
It's Okay to Fail

These past six months I've looked forward to my daily phone calls from Emily and live in anticipation of seeing her on a short break this summer. She always made me smile and laugh. I knew it must be hard on her and tried to be upbeat and positive, although I knew she and Aubrey talked every day and she must know of my difficulties.

Emily, Aubrey, and Matt were my heartbeat. I missed her, but I was happy she was back at school around her teammates and coaches. She helped with my memory and speech each day she called.

My speech had not improved. I still spoke in a monotone hoarse whisper difficult to understand... plus I put an 'a' sound at the end of my words. No one had said anything about it, but it saddened me. I saw the mountain I must climb and all the obstacles in my way. It's overwhelming.

Emily was reassuring. "It's okay to fail," Mom, it's part of the learning process." Her words were sympathetic, but strong.

PT was going better. I was determined to walk freely. OT was what it was. It was a slow process retraining this beautiful brain to do tasks of personal hygiene and self-care, but it's doable. I would get there. Speech, though. That was by far the most difficult process. I could see the words I wanted to say but could not connect the process.

Matt, Aubrey, and Emily allowed me to feel safe through trying to relearn.

They were there every day, every hour, every minute. They were there in the good times and the bad. Even knowing my faults, of which there are many, they were there to listen, to defend, to love. They understood my anxieties, my triggers, and the ghosts that haunted me. No matter how illogical I seemed, they kept me safe. They are the ones who always defended me, who were honest, who listened, and who cared. I won't always be able to communicate my wants, desires, needs; they may not always have the answers, but they will never let me be alone in my thoughts, in my sadness and despair. Was I worthy of such love and sacrifice? I pushed harder than I ever thought possible, to make them feel they were doing a great job which they were, no doubt. The only way I knew how to say "Thank you, I couldn't do this without you" was by showing them. This could not be about me! This had to be about everyone involved in this process. Team Pod!

Chapter 51

Sunday Mornings

Matt would often ask me, "Do you want to go back to church?"

"Yes!" I would say, then Sunday morning would roll around, and I would feel so embarrassed, so ashamed, so frightened that I would automatically break down in tears. Being out in public felt like the walls were closing in on me as I forced myself to take a step. We could be in a vast, open-air place, and if there were strangers there, my heart rate would race, my hands would sweat profusely, and my breathing would become short gasps. I will myself to lift my feet while using the walker, ashamed. My ears would shut down and my throat would tighten. I would become dizzy with fear.

Emotions. The very thing that makes us human. To be happy, have pride, joy, excitement, love and relief. We consider these emotions good. But

what would you be if you never felt
sadness, fear, hurt, pain, or despair?
You can't have the good without the
bad. There is no light without
darkness. The trick is to balance the
good and the bad, so the bad doesn't
seem permanent, so it doesn't seem so
terrible, and so you can appreciate
what is good and the beauty of each
day. Often, I reminded that it's okay to
emote, to mourn the person I once
was, but also to celebrate the new life
I had. The new me. I think some
people might refer to this as the
beginning and the end.

God separated the light from the
darkness. He called the light "day" and
the darkness he called "night."
Therefore, we are taught that there is
an evening and a morning. Both are
very important for embracing change.
Matt always addresses me without
anger or condemnation. I assume that
is where our daughters got their love
for living, for life, their compassion,
and empathy. He reminds me that, "I
feel God as keenly as the love I have

for you and our girls. If we can't trust our senses, then the whole notion of reality is up for grabs. He is Love; I feel His presence. I hope you can too." I felt safe around Matt and our daughters. I hoped someday I would look back and be able to see the beauty in the darkness. But today, I couldn't seem to find life out of fear.

I struggled with thinking of my present life with no foreseeable future. Today was a challenge. Another obstacle to face. Today. What happened yesterday? I tried to remember something... anything. Yesterday? What was on the agenda for tomorrow? If I wasn't careful, I could quickly get caught up in the uneasiness of emotions.

Matt realized what was going on with my thoughts. He reached over and held my hand, whispered in my ear and quietly said, "Maybe soon. Let's not push it. We can have our own church here where you feel safe." Then he leaned over and kissed me softly on the cheek.

The thought of being around a large group of people would easily scare me away. They reminded me that people used to energize me, but now, now I was an introvert, a frightened dog who had been beaten. I shook and tried to breathe.

I dreamed of being my old self. Freely moving, laughing in a large group, being silly. In my daydreams I turned like a child dancing in the breeze, twirling around, arms outstretched, face soaking up the sun. These were moves my mind could imagine but my body could not make. As I twirl, I was alone, enjoying sweet solitude, just the sound of the wind through the trees and the birds singing. But, my reality paints a different story. I live life from the safety of my home, for that was where my heart was, cocooned within the love of a strong family who freely gave their time to assist me. As much as I long for and dream of the freedom I once had, I had to find the fight to show my family I care. I might never be the person I once was. Now I had to figure out life in a new way. I wanted us all to have freedom once again.

Chapter 52
Tears Shed

I missed laughing. I missed Emily. Summer break had been short, and I wouldn't see her again until Christmas. She shared stories with me trying to trigger something I once had I used to love April Fool's day; I loved to make people laugh, I would include everyone.

Everyone is so serious, what happened, oh I remember, I died three times and declared brain dead. Come on, there is humor in that, and then these tears! I cry all the time. The doctor explained this was normal...normal to cry!

Remember when we would laugh so hard tears would roll down our red faces? Now, I'm afraid to share but must explain somehow tears are how I understand myself best. When I cry, I know who I really was. I am alive and that's better than dying and staying dead, right?

I cry when others hurt, and I feel sorry for myself. I cry at the brutal world news and sad movies. I cry during commercials. Tears are my strength and my weakness. Strength because it brings understanding and shows healing, we cannot see; weakness because who wants to always be with a weepy loved one? I wish I could turn my tears off, I do, or perhaps just save them until I'm alone. What's the saying? Oh, I think I remember: "When you laugh, the world laughs with you; when you cry, you cry alone." Wow, that's sad but probably true.

Somehow my brain had been rewired. My emotions swirled like a whirlpool, deep and strong. Sometimes I was scared to dive in case I didn't make it out again, but I couldn't be anyone else. So, for now, I would embrace these emotions, this empathy I had somehow been gifted with, and freely love this minute as I was watching my husband make dinner again.

Chapter 53
Red Like Roses

Thank goodness Matt was a great cook... he was a great catch! I wondered if he knew how much I was grateful for his sacrifices. Matt came over and set down bowls of green pasta, green salad, lime Jell-O and honeydew melon! Green.

I looked at all the green and tried to focus. I had to tell him I wanted red foods now, but I would close my eyes and pretend to see red. I see red roses, red rosy cheeks, red pasta sauce, raspberry jam. What a beautiful color. I would ask him after dinner. Red. I hoped this stopped soon. I smiled and with the biggest grin said, "Thank you!"

We transferred to the living room and Matt turned on Downton Abbey, a safe show we enjoy watching together. Matt poured himself a scotch and handed me a hot tea. The smell of scotch was repulsive and assaulted my senses. I guessed he had a drink after I go to bed, trying to wind down from our hectic days. I hoped it helped him. He and Aubrey were both working hard to do everything possible to help me.

Chapter 54
Silence

Another Day. Early in the morning, after a very long night shift, Aubrey had breakfast ready. She and Matt went over the days' agenda. They loaded me into the car, and I sat in silence. I could tell Aubrey was tired today and so was I. We had been on this schedule for a long time with no end in sight.

We arrived at rehab and our first appointment was speech therapy.

Katie spoke to Aubrey, who was my confidante and my voice. Her understanding of what to do to help me breaks my heart. Her twenty-first birthday was this year.

Many celebrations had come and gone while the focus was always on me. The thought of this made me very sad. I looked at her while Katie was explaining something rather important about my speech. Aubrey explained that I was working hard with all my homework and she thought I was doing a good job. Katie was concerned at not seeing much improvement over the past eight months.

It was Aubrey's compassion that was the bridge to understanding what I needed. She was always the first one to volunteer to help. She extended her hand to hold mine. She understood the scars I carried, the mess and the fear. She reached over and held me close, let me hide in her words, in her hug. Every time I thought she had had enough, there was only patience I never felt I'd earned. I never wanted it to be this way.

I am the mom. I needed to be strong, though I haven't been and was still so far from it. True healing takes time; there are no magic wands for deep pain. I hoped she would find a sense of completion. I would try to be more diligent with therapy. No promises, but you know me by now: my word means something, or it used to when I could talk. Now I must show my resolve by actions.

Therapy was always exhausting and overstimulating. As soon as we got home Aubrey tucked me back into bed, in the quiet, in the darkened room. She lay down with me and began telling stories of her days. Of her friends. I laughed when she laughed.

I lay there in wonder thinking of our daughters. Both were a precious gift, just as precious as a beautiful jewel, a diamond. God has made many diamonds, but none like them. Each of us are unique, and they were my beautiful diamonds capable of reflecting the light with such vibrancy as to remind me of the stars on a cloudless night, full of its rarity and beauty. Our girls were a symbol of purity and innocence, of love and fidelity that embraced strength of character, ethics, and faithfulness to oneself and others.

It showed the loving and open nature with which they had blessed us and encouraged truth and trust. They were entitled to make as many mistakes as any other and still be a full recipient of family love. How the tides had turned. I used to take care of them, nurturing and loving and now they were taking care of me with the same love and nurturing to my soul.

Our oldest had put her life on hold. My twenty-year-old daughter, my smart, athletic girl, she chose to help. No one was forcing her; she had freely given up her time, her life, her dreams for my sake, my safety! How would I ever make this up to her?

I smiled at Aubrey, a warm pink hue lighting up the room, dancing rhythmically around each breath as she lay her head on Dad's pillow and quietly drifted to sleep. I lay watching her, not wanting to close my eyes for fear of missing this moment. Her heavy breathing was hypnotic and soon I fell asleep next to her.

.

Chapter 55

I'm Here!

I woke screaming, "I'm okay, I'm here!"

Matt bolted into the bedroom and rushed to my side. "You are safe, sweetie, you are safe now!" He exclaimed, winded.

He sat on the bed and helped me sit up, wiping the sweat and tears from my face. "Aubrey didn't want to wake you. She left for work as soon as I came home," Matt said cautiously, making sure not to overstimulate this brain injury.

"You're okay now?" he asked.

I nodded my head yes.

"Are you hungry? I bought red food for dinner and breakfast. It smells delicious, doesn't it?"

I nodded my head yes.

"Use your words!"

"Yes." I replied.

Matt helped me get up and get ready for dinner. We made our way to the dining room. The table was set for two. Fresh stemless red roses graced the table; a red candle flickered in the center. It looked like raspberry lemonade for me and a cold beer for Matt. Matt seated me, then placed a napkin on my lap and tucked one in my lapel. This created a burst of laughter from both of us.

Laughter! What a great gift. To laugh uncontrollably is the best way to spend time with those you love. I didn't remember how or why I laughed so hard, but suddenly, I couldn't stop. Matt was laughing with me. Both of us were unsure what caused the outburst. Our breath came in quick gasps between my unstoppable giggles. Tears gathered in the corners of our eyes, spilling over our rosy cheeks.

"Oh, my Mary, you make this life better than I deserve. You work so hard in getting your abilities back, you smile when you see me and for this, I am forever grateful. I love you, my silly lady!

"I've given Aubrey the weekend off. Just you and me. Let me know if you want to do something special, otherwise I have strict instructions from our oldest to keep you on your scheduled homework." Matt raised his eyebrow if scolding me in a playful way.

After dinner I enjoyed a cup of hot tea with the tincture and go tucked into bed. The dreams were just that, dreams. I tried not to remember any of them, but I knew the nightmares were not as intense. All because of a few drops of an herb that only a few states allow. Thank goodness Colorado was one of those states. Thank you, God, for allowing me to live.

Saturday morning greeted me with a delicious breakfast. The moment Matt helped me sit in the chair he pushed me to the table with the sound of a train pulling up a hill, "Chugga, chugga, choo- choo!"

He served me an enormous platter of red food mixed with the orange color. Eggs with melted cheddar cheese and finely chopped tomatoes, fresh strawberries, a glass of V-8 juice, and pastries filled with strawberry jam.

Matt had the biggest smile on his face. "I know, I know Mary. So much food, but I am enjoying cooking for us! I guess I got carried away."

I smiled at his beautiful grin and hoarsely said, "Thank you!"

Chapter 56
Butterflies

"After breakfast let's get started on your homework. Aubrey said it's important to stay on schedule. Speech, physical therapy, and then lastly occupational therapy. Is that right?" Matt asked.

I nodded yes.

"Oh, she also said to make you use your words, no nodding or pointing." He looked at me, concerned making sure I understood.

"Yes," I said.

Okay, now he was smiling, which brought out my smile. We've been married for twenty years and sometimes I felt we had just met. Butterflies and all. Matt loves me. I wondered if our girls saw it. How great was our love, to love even in times of trouble, of hardship, or medically life-altering situation like ours?

315

Matt is a special man whom I am thankful for. No matter what curveball is thrown our way, he shows more grace than many do in times of trouble. It is in those moments of pain and fear I see right to his heart and know that my faith in him, my love for him, is forever. I am forever yours. You are a brave, kind, always giving of yourself. I want you to know that I will be the same for you; I will be your mirror, bring to you what you give others—true love, the lasting kind. Although I couldn't say those words, I know my brain is actively trying to communicate. How odd is it to see the words I wanted to say, to articulate my feelings, to use the romance of words? What he does for me, for our family doesn't escape me.

Matt helped me get ready for the day. He applied a large glob of toothpaste on my toothbrush and did the same with his. "Ready?" he asked.

We picked up our brushes. "It's not a race. Let's practice together." Matt's smile was all the encouragement I needed.

Brushing my teeth was messy. I didn't remember it being so messy. I leaned over the sink and closed my lips over the toothbrush only to have the foam from brushing spill out over the sink, my mouth, and down the front of my shirt. Messy. I looked up at Matt, rather embarrassed, and he was smiling.

"Doing great, sweetheart. We will finish in another 90 seconds and then we can clean up."

Ninety seconds! Ninety. Matt explained: 30 seconds lower right, 30 seconds lower left, 30 seconds upper right, and finish with 30 seconds upper left.

Two minutes of continuous brushing. Two minutes of standing hunched over a sink. Two minutes of standing. Two minutes. You can do this. Lean over the sink. Rest your hand on the porcelain basin. Remain standing. You can do this. It's only two minutes. Focus.

Almost there, almost. I was curious; had I always given myself these little pep talks?

Speech therapy was next. He escorted me to our dining room table. Matt brought out the cards, and we went through them slowly. His patience was very encouraging. He held up the red card and asked, "What color is this, Mary?" So businesslike. I took on his studious attitude and worked diligently at staying focused.

"Red a," I stammer.

Matt remembered what the speech therapist, Katie, had explained to him. Patients with brain injuries often have dysarthria, a speech impediment that put an extra sound at the end of words. One way to help was to focus on words that have similar sounds. Matt skipped the colors and begin writing.

"Let's see if this will help." He was so serious, like he was trying to solve a problem that had taken too long to fix.

He filled the first page with simple words.

While I studied the words, he looked through the cards and pulled out several that had pictures which represented the words: Bat, Cat, Hat, Mat, Rat, Sat.

"Okay, let's do this together."

I focused and said, "Bat a."

Matt said, "Bat, can you say BAT?"

"Bat a!" I repeated.

Matt patiently repeated what I had said, "Bat a? Let's make it simple: Bat. Now your turn."

"Bat a," I said in my hoarse monotone whisper.

Matt didn't miss a beat. Next card was a cat. "Mary, can you tell me what this is?" He asked patiently.

"Cat a," I said.

"C A T." Matt was sure to pronounce every letter. "Can you repeat after me? KAA AAA TTT."

"KA A T a," I tried.

Forty-five minutes later with no success, Matt shows no signs of discouragement. He made several notes and then we moved on to PT. Aubrey had showed him the walking video we were working with. Matt hung on tightly to my gait belt and settled us in front of the TV.

"Mary, I would feel more comfortable having your walker in front of you as we practice. I realize this may seem like a setback, but we have to work together," Matt said cautiously. "Do you understand?"

I began to nod my head as Matt began shaking his no. "Use your words," he said.

"Yes," I said in agreement.

He found the Leslie Sansone YouTube walking videos. He helped me stand and placed the walker in sight but not close enough to use it as a crutch. We began walking in place, trying to keep pace with the rhythmic sounds, the hypnotic beat. Ten minutes in, it exhausted me. My ears were shutting down and so was I. Matt sensed this and stopped the video. "You did so good, honey! Soon we will walk outside."

We had begun with OT; we would finish with OT. "Let's get you showered and dressed. I'll help, but I really want to see what you can do on your own."

Matt grabbed his pen and paper and began taking notes on our PT.

We walked to the bathroom. By the time we got there I was exhausted. Matt pulled up a chair.

"Honey! Is that the farthest you have walked without the walker? You are doing great."

PT seemed the easiest of the three. Though I had a long way to go, I didn't mind putting in the extra work.

OT was difficult but manageable.

Speech was always defeating.

I felt insurmountably sad, confused, and frustrated.

I tried to hide this side of me. I often thought of my family and how this had affected them. Emily called every day and asked me to tell her something about my day. Speaking was the hardest, waking up the diaphragm and using my vocal cords. I always smiled when I saw her number, but I just wanted to listen to her stories, her voice.

Chapter 57
Jesus is the Light

As we worked out a routine, I grew more in love with Matt, with his gentle care and the uncanny ability to make me laugh even on the cold days of confusion. When I felt lost, he always searched for me in the darkness of my mind, providing the needed physical touch and soothing voice. He loved me even when I couldn't love myself. I think of Jesus the same way. When we are lost, which everyone will be at some point, Jesus is the light that provides comfort and healing, whether it is physical or spiritual. I don't know where we would be without faith. When I listened to other people share their experiences, I could quickly discern a person of faith from those who don't believe. Their colors were different. I stayed clear when I saw an ominous sheer black aura. That scared me.

As I learned how to shuffle around the house without the use of the walker,

Matt and Aubrey always made sure I was not alone, always working their schedules around my care. I can't imagine how challenging that was. Our twenty-year-old daughter putting her life on hold, her dreams on the back burner, to do everything workable to care for me. Me.

Learning how to become independent seemed impossible, defeating. Looking at the big picture was staggering. I had to learn how to live in the moment. To breathe. As simple as that seems, at that point in my journey it would freeze me, scare me.

Yet, the sooner I became independent, the sooner our daughters could figure their lives out.

Time went on.

Chapter 58

That's What She Said

I tried my best to use my words.

Laughter was a genuine gift, and I was blessed with many opportunities. I would usually laugh at myself, which is the best way to relax and not get anxious about perfection. Matt, Aubrey, and Emily joined in on the fun. It got so ridiculous that Matt kept a journal of what I said and what he heard. This is a copy of the actual document.

What she said	What he heard
Another pot roast	I'm not a pyro
Will you call or text as much as you can?	Will you call a taxi you think is a can?
I have all your delicates in my bathroom.	I have all your delicates on my bottom.

I like having a productive day.	I like having a dark, dark face.
Did you put the soap in?	Did you leave this open?
I'd like to know what the scores are.	I like the wild forest signs.
They have a live harpist.	They have alive carpets.
The bottom line, I don't want them to drink anymore.	Vodka and lime will make me not look anymore.
Vegetables	French dimples
I need to find a way to relax tonight.	I need to find a way to get locked in ice.
Are you and Tak roommates again, Matt?	Do you want to toss mace again, Matt?
I have regular socks on.	I want to own a sod farm.

Because of my black eye	I'm a black guy
I just need to get socks and shoes on.	I just need to have sex with Susha
Rose hasn't posted a comment	Rose got to get back to the convent.
Do you have Heads Up on your phone?	Hashtag macaroni salad

I hope you can find joy, a little bit of laughter, when reading this.

Chapter 59

God Blessed Us with Humor

One day on the way to outpatient rehabilitation, Aubrey was singing "The Hairbrush Song" from VeggieTales. I tried to sing along.

"Oha Where is mya hairbrush..."

Aubrey laughed so hard; tears sprung from her eyes.

I painstakingly shared my words. "Aubrey, I'm glad that God never took away my sense of humor!"

"Mom," Aubrey said, laughing while driving, "I'm glad he finally gave you one!"

I laughed so hard, so freely, so normally. Normal. I felt normal for the first time in so long. Normal. I lost myself in Aubrey's presence. Her sure beauty was deep. She was my light.

"Aubrey, the doctor thinks I should get a service dog. Did Dad tell you?" I tried to enunciate my words.

"Yes! I think it's a great idea, Mom. I'll help you with the dog until you can care for it on your own." She said with hope.

"Dad gave me his report on your in-home rehab. You are doing great! I am so proud of you!"

I lost my thought process then. Aubrey drove us to rehab in silence.

Rehab was the same. Trying... trying... trying... failing... failing... failing. M-W-F.

T-TH home therapy with Aubrey.

Saturdays with Matt.

Sundays a day of rest and recovery.

Chapter 60
Same Old Story, Same Old Me

Months passed by. Physically, I was doing much better. I still used the walker, but Aubrey and I took short walks outside with just the gait belt.

We used the video Emily made for me before heading back to school. I still use it today. Getting up and down was a no-go, so after talking with Aubrey about my struggles, Emily made me an exercise video using a balance ball. She added weights to help build muscle and explained that exercise was great for brain health. She claimed I had to reevaluate my goals. I should work out and try art therapy for brain health. I shouldn't cloud the process. Everything had a purpose. My purpose should be brain health, anything else is a bonus.

Matt and I went for walks outside after dinner. We are slowly making our way through this journey together. Sometimes I used a walker and sometimes we shuffled our way around with the help of the gait belt.

Chapter 61

Garden of The Gods

Feeling adventurous, Matt and I went to The Garden of The Gods park on a beautiful fall day. Emily was back in school, starting her junior year. Aubrey was taking a night class at a community college while working and taking care of my needs. The snow on the crest of Pikes Peak, America's mountain, reflected the sunshine. The air was crisp, with a cloud covered sky. A perfect day.

"Mary, do you trust me?"

I looked at Matt, confused by the question.

His eyes glimmered with hope. "Well, do you?"

"Yes." I replied, curious.

"I want us to walk together, without the walker. I know it will scare you to be in public without the security of hanging on, but I want to be your security today. We can go as slowly as you want, rest when you want, come back when you want. I want you to experience the freedom you once had, we once had."

Through misty eyes, I agreed.

Freedom? Matt had one arm around my waist. The other guided me and held on to my left arm, helping control the movement. I needed to do this for him. He knew it was a lot to ask, but his confidence in my ability was all I needed, all I needed to survive this outing, to make him proud, to make him laugh, smile, and see me for the person I used to be.

We shuffled around the park, stopping at every bench, taking in the sun, the fresh air. I didn't want to leave. I could have stayed there, in his arms, his presence.

We made our way to a bench along the paved parkway. Painfully slowly. We were so slow a blind man passed us with his walking stick. People with disabilities can be capable but this chap could have been preparing for a marathon. I watched in awe and admiration. He didn't let his blindness stop him from living. (Sigh) I had a long way to go.

"You did it!" Matt clapped like a child who has just won his first board game.

"We did it together!" I slowly muttered in my hoarse tone of what was left of any energy I once had. "We did it!" I tried to match his smile, but his smile was a beaming light and mine, well, must be a smile of gratitude.

I made sure I had my balance, then I looked up at Matt, who had tears falling from his brilliant eyes. He leaned in for a kiss which unsteadied me, but Matt caught me before I fell.

Matt asked me carefully, "Honey, your speech is not getting better. Katie said that your diaphragm and vocal cords are still lethargic, sleepy. She has explained that you can see the words but are having a difficult time finding your voice. Do you feel this is accurate?"

The bench was cold; I was uncomfortable. The thought of never being able to speak to communicate again did not scare me. It seemed comforting not having to talk. Speech was difficult, defeating. I shrugged my shoulders.

"I have an idea. I am not sure if it will work, but if you are up for it, I would like to begin when we get home." His eyes, his smile was inviting; his love was my strength.

"Okay" I said in my damaged whisper.

Matt leaned over, wrapped his arms around me, kissed the top of my head, and whispered, "I could sit here with you until old age takes us both, but we have work to do." He leaned forward to look in my eyes. "I am so glad you stayed."

We drove off in our little black two-door Honda Civic. Matt buckled me in, strapping my left arm into the seatbelt to prevent me the embarrassment of trying to control it on my own. No handholding, no words. Matt was deep in thought. Staring at his chiseled features was relaxing. I became drowsy. I enjoy sleeping in the car: something so familiar, so comfortable. The rhythmic sound of silence, beautiful, peaceful silence. I closed my eyes and fell asleep in the tranquility of safety.

Matt gently woke me up after we pulled into the garage. He unleashed my left side from the seatbelt. He reached over to help me out of the car. As he stood me up, I "accidentally" smacked his bottom.

He looked astonished. "You did that on purpose!"

I shrugged my shoulders and tried my best to form a wink.

He escorted me into our home and sat me down by the window with the view of the evergreen trees, the snow-capped mountains, the songbirds. He draped a blanket over my lap and headed for the kitchen to make a late lunch, an early dinner. Chicken pasta salad. Colorless.

.

Chapter 62
Elves or...

I noticed how clean the house was but couldn't remember anyone taking the time to clean. Had Matt hired a cleaning service? We were never out of healthy food. Our household was carefully orchestrated to be stress free for me, for us. But who did all this? Magical elves? The thought made me laugh.

Matt leaned over the kitchen counter. "What are you laughing at? Wait, you're laughing! You're laughing! Are you laughing or crying?" A bit panicked, he rushed over to me. "Honey, are you okay? What happened?"

"Do we have elves?" I whispered out loud.

"Elves?" Matt repeated, "Do we have elves?" Concerned I was seeing things. Everything that could go wrong was streaming through his thoughts. He put his hand on my head to see if I was running a fever.

"So clean," I said, smiling.

Matt sat down next to me and held me tightly. I knew I scared him. I didn't know how gingerly he was living his life. He had placed his life in first gear up a steep incline. His once-active life was now going at my pace. My slow pace. I didn't realize how his life I burdened with fear.

"Honey, do you see elves?" he asked, concerned.

"No. Who cleans and shops? Is it elves?" I replied laboriously, wanting to assure him I was okay.

Matt carefully repeated what he heard. "No. Who cleans and shops?" He realized I was laughing at my own thoughts. He could not contain his smile!

"Aubrey is our elf. She is home, probably cleaning downstairs. She went grocery shopping while we were out. It's Aubrey, sweetie," Matt said with pride, gratitude.

I listened carefully and heard singing in the distance. What was she singing? "I Love My Lips"? I looked at Matt and he began singing along. "Aubrey is your sweet girl, isn't she, sweetie?"

"Aubrey, Aubrey the elf!" I chuckled.

"After we eat, I want to try something if you are up for it." Matt winked playfully. "The food is almost ready. Do you mind if I play the piano while we wait?"

My eyes lit up. "Yes!"

.

Chapter 63
Music Therapy

Matt made his way to our grand piano. It was too big for the room, but it was a beautiful piece of our history together: Matt playing, working out new songs, my own private concerts. I wondered to myself when he had last performed with his bands. How long had he put his love for music, his lifeline, on hold to care for me?

I listened as I applauded him with my  eyes. I tried to clap, but I couldn't control my left side. I imagined a cymbal-banging monkey toy whose rhythm was off. Once again, I laughed. Tears of peace, the joy of love. Each note he played brought memories of our lives together. That's the thing about music, it didn't save my life, but it gave me strength in the memories.

Our grand piano is made of walnut wood. The curves are elegant, shapely and have many stories to share. Our story might be its last. Matt played on the real ivory and ebony keys; he plays the out-of-tune keys as if he were playing on a Steinway. It's about loving something and seeing past its flaws to create something beautiful. He was gentle and careful.

I stared at my husband as he became lost in his music. He shimmered with a sparkling aura of purple, blue, and yellow. It took my breath away. The sounds he was creating, the music, were wonders to my soul. Such elegance, the balance of beauty and pain, of hope and fear.

He recently shared with me he has saved every note I put in his lunches. Everyone. He couldn't make out what they said, but that was okay. It meant a lot to him that Aubrey, and I took the time to do this for him. A daily reminder of my love.

When Matt played for me it felt as though his music was teaching my brain to communicate, to wake up, to breathe, to listen, to love, to live in peace. When he played and slowly changed tone it massaged my auditory skills, the part that someone had told me the damage was irreversible, the part my medical team thought was permanently gone. I had accepted that I could never communicate again, that language was lost, gone forever. But Matt believed he could help me. He saw the beauty in my thought process, in my trying. He and our girls never gave up, even when I did. They never ceased to believe.

Matt played softly, inviting me to feel the presence, the find the ever-patient version of me, the one who was afraid to be seen, to speak, to be heard. He was coaxing me with his music, allowing me the safety of being in the present.

He looked over his left shoulder as his fingers caressed the keys, playing by memory. He glimpsed over at me in the sunlight, saw the redness of my nose and my cheeks and rushed to me once again.

"Honey, Mary, are you okay? What's wrong? Are you hurt?"

I shook my head no.

"Use your words, please tell me!"

"Beautiful!" I said and reached for his hands.

"Are you ready for our experiment?" he asked.

"I want to listen to you play," I tried to communicate.

"Perfect! I will walk you over to the chair next to the piano and we will read *Green Eggs and Ham* to the music. You will match the pitch of the keys as you read the words," Matt said excitedly.

Bright-eyed, I looked at him. His excitement was contagious. "Okay!"

After making sure I was comfortable: blanket over my lap, book in hand, he sat down and stared at the ivory keys, contemplating the story he had memorized. He recited the first two pages and asked me to follow along. "Sam I am," he said. "Sam I am. Sam, I am. I do not like that Sam I am!"

He took his right hand and hit the key of C. "Sam."

I tried: "Sam a," in a hushed monotone whisper.

"Again, try to match the pitch of the keys, sweetie." Matt began to hum the key of C. I mimicked him. I was humming! Actually humming!

"Almost." He played a C again and said, "Sam."

"Sam!" I said in the key of C.

You would have thought we had won the lottery. Matt's excitement was incredible. "That's right, Sam in the key of C!"

"Sam a! Sam a! Sam a!" I sang in the

key of C. "Sam!"

Matt wasn't so concerned about the added vowel sound. It overjoyed him to help me wake my diaphragm and use my voice. It took lots of patience, but he never stopped believing in music as therapy for us both.

We focused on music and speech for many months. Music therapy and reading out loud would become part of our Saturday home therapy schedule, one I enjoyed. Soon, I could read the entire *Green Eggs and Ham* book out loud.

We often joke that he taught me how to speak again but forgot to teach me how to shut up!

Five days a week, Aubrey and I would make his lunch and five days a week I would send him a love note, continuing to work on my handwriting and thought process.

Love Note. The play on words didn't escape me. Matt was teaching me diction and to vary my tone using musical notes as I practiced penmanship by writing him notes. Love Note. Yup, that described us. Matt shared that his favorite part of the day was finding notes in his lunchbox.

Chapter 64
Going Back

On a chilly fall day, as I was approaching the one-year anniversary of my death (or was it life?), Matt asked how I was doing. I didn't reply. So many celebrations had gone by. How could I possibly celebrate the moment in time that had forever changed our paths?

He told me that on November 21 we would visit the hospital where I spent so many days in the wilderness. He would show me where family and friends had camped out. We would say thank you to those who had cared for me. Matt made the thank you cards for us to hand out.

I asked to go to bed early. My thoughts were overwhelming. Fear was creeping in on me again. Fear was a hopeless sensation. I felt like I was drowning and there was no hope of being saved. The blackness of my memories started to spread through my mind, clouding my thoughts and taking me back to places I never wanted to revisit. And now, I was going back to where the bad had begun. Where death tried to be victorious. Where my nightmares began. I pressed my palms to my ears, my mouth, trying to block out the screams, but it didn't work. They only grew louder and louder. I just wanted them to go away. Was that too much to ask?

Just when I thought I lost all hope, I heard Matt's voice calling my name. "Mary, Mary, I'm here. Listen to my voice. I'm here!" It was like a ray of light in the darkness of my past. It guided me back to reality. I felt him take my hands in his and pull me into his arms as though I were a child. The screams died down. Matt told me that everything was all right, that it was all just a distant memory. I rested my head on his chest. He was my anchor. He gave me hope when darkness creeped in, when fear tried to be my only friend.

I then realized the date. November 21.

I hadn't expected the magnitude of gratitude that we would both show. Everyone remembered Matt, remembered how careful he was with me, how he always had someone with me in case I would wake up. The staff was so encouraged by my progress. Progress? I was still using a walker part of the time. My memory had been greatly affected. My speech, although getting better, was soft and difficult to understand. Yet everyone celebrated.

I didn't understand until one of the ICU nurses explained that she would often search the obituaries for me. No one, not one person who had cared for me, expected any recovery, so seeing me gave them hope.

Chapter 65

Hope

We got home, and I mentally shut down. I needed a small quiet place to decompress. Matt asked if I just wanted to sit in the car for a while. I couldn't speak. My throat had closed; my ears had shut down. I only shook my head and turned away. The tears fell, and I didn't know how to stop them.

Matt tenderly held my hand. "It is hard today, isn't it? I mean hearing the stories from the staff, the people who were so happy to see you. I have saved every single note you have written, every single one of them. I witnessed the challenges in your handwriting. Every obstacle you face, we face together."

I could only nod my head in agreement.

"When we return to relive those moments, we learn that our present becomes a part of our history. Do you understand?" Matt said patiently. "This conversation will become a part of our history. But the beautiful part of any ending is that we always get a new beginning, a chance to start over."

I turned towards him and focused on his words, his understanding.

"Mary, honey, we just may discover that winning over our troubles and struggles is our greatest treasure. Therefore, today, as difficult as it was, was a victory. We should celebrate! How about a beer?" He grinned in his magnificent way and winked at me.

I stared lovingly into his eyes and inquired, "Matt, would you play the piano for me, create our own Love Note?"

He kissed me on my forehead and said, "It's time to go in now!'

Picture from November 2014 of Matt and Mary

{Acknowledgements}

This started when Matt kept everyone abreast of the dire situation using a blog, he created titled, "Mary Kaye's Odyssey." You can read the blog in our first book, "Broken Hallelujah 40 Days in The Wilderness."

In his last line he had suggested that MK finish the story.

So many people from around the world reach out and wanted to know how I was doing which then, our dear friend Brenda Schaeffer said, "You need to write a book."

I could barely hang on to a thought and the risk of writing was scary. But with continued art therapy we began a two-year long journey and published "Broken Hallelujah, 40 Days in The Wilderness." The response was incredibly encouraging.

This is a continuation of that time in our lives as we pick up the story from leaving the rehabilitation facility to our one-year anniversary.

I'm still in Art Therapy and my thought process is clearer but I will always have a brain injury. I will always have a disability. Just like I will always believe, always have faith, a strong family and supportive friends.

Life changes in an instant. Thank you for taking the time to be part of our journey, our story.

Compassion is a key element to success. We have been blessed with such an amazing family.

Our niece, Alex, is studying health care, whether that be a nurse, a doctor or a therapist. This experience has put her on an unexpected path.

Kennedy is study engineering. She will make people's lives better.

MK and Matt Podschweit

Share your love notes with someone special.

Just in case

I have yet to

Tell you today

I love you

(Write your love note here)

I Love you

More Everyday

(Write your love note here)

I'm Your greatest fan!

(Write your love note here)

When I think of you...

I smile as if it were the first time our eyes met

.

You Make My Heart Sing

Write your love note here)

I appreciate you and everything you do for us.

(Write your love note here)

Thank you for....

Loving

Me

I can't imagine life without you.

I love the way you trust God.

I am glad that God gave you to me.

.

You make my heart sing!

(write your love note here)

In a world that can become dark, you are my light and I love you.

[1]For more information, refer to: Connelly, Thomas P. "Why We Take Medicines Under Our Tongue." HuffPost. HuffPost, May 25, 2011. https://www.huffpost.com/entry/medicine-in-the-body-_b_823530?guccounter=1.

Notes

_____

Made in the USA
Columbia, SC
29 September 2021